More
Than
Bread

More Than Bread

Ethnography of a Soup Kitchen

by Irene Glasser

The University of Alabama Press

Tuscaloosa and London

Library of Congress Cataloging-in-Publication Data

Glasser, Irene.
    More than bread.
    Bibliography: p.
    Includes index.
    1. Relief stations (for the poor)—Social aspects—United
States.   2. Poor—United States—Social conditions.   3. Poverty—
Psychological aspects.   I. Title.
HV696.S6G42   1988   362.5′8′0973   87-34264
ISBN 0-8173-0397-9 (alk. paper)

British Library Cataloguing-in-Publication Data is available.

Book design by Kathleen Giencke.
Illustrations by Jason Glasser.

To my parents, Charlotte and Gerald Biederman; my sons, Jason, Raphael, Jonathan, and Nathaniel; and my husband, Morty.

Contents

List of Tables   viii
Acknowledgments   ix
1   The Contemporary Soup Kitchen   1
2   A Historical Perspective   14
3   The Tabernacle Soup Kitchen   23
4   Field Study Methods   34
5   Profile of the Guest Population   49
6   Loneliness   69
7   An Ambience of Acceptance   86
8   Social Networks and Social Support   100
9   Self-Help in the Dining Room: Guests as
     Counselors   118
10   Staff Philosophy and the Concept of Ministry   138
11   Concluding Thoughts   150
References   162
Index   176

Tables

5.1   Results of Brief Survey of 104 Guests   51

5.2   Demographic Characteristics of Surveyed Guests   54

5.3   Source of Income   57

5.4   Housing Problems Reported   58

5.5   Health Issues Reported by Surveyed Soup Kitchen Guests   59

5.6   Guests with Mental Health Problems   61

5.7   Missing Food Groups in Diet Recalls   67

8.1   Map of the Tabernacle Soup Kitchen at 11 A.M.   102

Acknowledgments

I would like to thank the guests of the Tabernacle Soup Kitchen for their generosity and time in helping me understand life in the dining room. I thank Jane Suroviak of Lebanon, Connecticut, for her daily demonstration of leadership in the soup kitchen community.

I am especially indebted to Perti Pelto, director of the Program in Medical Anthropology at the University of Connecticut, for his support and guidance in the soup kitchen research. His belief in the mix of qualitative and quantitative methods has enabled me to describe life in a soup kitchen in what I hope is the fullest way possible.

I thank Robert Bee, professor in anthropology at the University of Connecticut, whose expertise in ethnography was valuable to my own descriptions. Robert Ness, professor in anthropology at the Medical College of Georgia, and Gerard Rowe-Minaya of the University of Connecticut offered their support and friendship in conducting the study of the Tabernacle Soup Kitchen.

I also enjoyed the friendship and stimulating conversations about the soup kitchen with Mikko Salo, professor in social policy and philosophy, University of Joensuu, Finland, during the year he was a visiting professor in Connecticut.

I would like to thank my friends and colleagues at Eastern Connecticut State University for their help and support, including Doris Griscom, Jody Newmyer, Blanche Blum, and Edith Mavor. I would like to thank my friends Susan Webb, Linda Heller, Donna Newton, and Jane Blanshard for all their goodwill. I thank my friends and colleagues at the University of Connecticut Department of Anthropology, including Jackie Bradley and Jean Wynn.

The Lauter Foundation provided support for the three courses in community counseling in the soup kitchen, and their help is gratefully acknowledged.

I would like to thank the Eastern Connecticut State University Foundation for their support during the writing of the book.

I thank my son Jason for his lovely illustrations of life in the soup kitchen. I thank my loving family for all of their support and encouragement throughout my work. I thank my parents, Charlotte and Gerald Biederman; my brother Michael; my niece, Francine Casale; my children Jason, Raphael, Jonathan, and Nathaniel; and my husband Morty, who was never too tired to hear, once again, what was new in the world of the soup kitchen.

Finally, I thank Judith Knight, chief editor, and Ellen Stein, assistant editor, of The University of Alabama Press for their help and advice.

More
Than
Bread

1

The Contemporary Soup Kitchen

It was snowing the day of George's memorial service. Most of the twenty or so people present were from the Tabernacle Soup Kitchen. The service was held in the small chapel above the soup kitchen, in Saint Mary's Church. George had died the previous week, and his obituary consisted of two sentences: one announcing his death, the other identifying the minister who would officiate at the memorial service.

George was a soup kitchen "regular." He was a black man in his fifties, tall, thin, with long matted hair and torn clothing. His eyes were always bloodshot, his beard grew in many directions, his gait was slow, and he stuttered. Often he could be seen walking on the streets between the west end of town and Main Street. He liked to stop and rest on the low stone wall of the First State Bank. George had been receiving dialysis treatment several times a week at a hospital in a neighboring town, and white gauze was visible around his wrists, under his oversized coat. I first met him in the spring of 1983 at the soup kitchen. I remember how solemn and dignified he seemed, and at the time I was conscious of trying not to disturb his meal; I sensed, and later confirmed, that this was to be his sole meal of the day.

At George's memorial service, the minister faced the group and said that we were gathered together to commemorate George

Smith's life and death. Since the minister had not known him personally, he read from small pieces of paper people had given to him to remember George:

> "I will always remember George's friendly smile and soft giggle as he greeted people from the wall of the bank."

> "I will always remember that as down and out as George looked and seemed to be, he always carried himself with respect and dignity."

Jane, a woman who had a severe motor impairment and was considered mentally slow, had taken the morning off from her sheltered workshop to attend the service. She read a psalm to the group. Alan, a balding thin man with a large bump on his forehead, gave the eulogy. He said that George's friendliness was outstanding, and he even liked the way George mispronounced his last name (referring to George's speech problems). At that point I noticed a large young man with long red hair, who usually sat by himself at the soup kitchen and was considered violent by the rest of the guests. He was seated several pews in front of me and was shaking all over throughout the service. Although I had never seen the man speak with George, he too was there to mourn George's death. Barbara, a soup kitchen worker on welfare, whose upper arms were tattooed with flowers, appeared to be an organizer of the ceremony. She handed everyone a copy of "Amazing Grace," which we sang at the end of the service. None of George's family seemed to be there.

After the ceremony, as people were leaving to go back downstairs to the soup kitchen, I tried to find out if anyone knew how George had died. No one did. Once downstairs, a group of men continued discussing his death. One said he thought the weather must have contributed to it.

What is the nature and significance of the soup kitchen, which had become in George's life and death the very center of his social existence? The soup kitchen may be seen as a particular adaptation to contemporary North American life, serving as an ecological niche for a segment of the poor who are considered "marginal" to the dominant culture. This marginality takes the forms of little income, long-term unemployment, debilitating physical conditions, serious mental illness, and a separation from family relationships. Because of these conditions, soup kitchen guests lack the sources of human contact that most of us take for granted in work, family relationships, and consumer activities. The soup kitchen functions as a symbolic living room for this segment of people in poverty, in a manner reminiscent of "Tally's Corner" for a group of urban men in Washington, D.C. (Liebow 1967), and the tavern for alcoholic men (Dumont 1967: 938–45).

The Tabernacle Soup Kitchen (a pseudonym) began in 1981 and is one of the thousands that have emerged in the United States in the last ten years. It is located in Middle City, a small industrialized city of 20,000 people in a New England state. The soup kitchen serves a hot meal to approximately one hundred men, women, and children, six days a week, fifty-two weeks a year. The doors of the soup kitchen are open from 8:30 A.M., when the large pot of coffee is first turned on, to 1 P.M., when the kitchen workers put the chairs on the table and the soup kitchen is over for the day. It is housed in the basement of a church, which gives it an underground quality in both a figurative and a literal sense. In Philip Slater's terms (1970: 21), the soup kitchen guests are out of sight and out of mind for the rest of the community.

The soup kitchen offers its guests a unique configuration of physical comforts and opportunities for sociability and acceptance in ways that are culturally congruent with its diners' life-styles. It provides such physical comforts as doughnuts, coffee, a hot meal, and bathrooms, along with a public meeting place where people can come together and leave at will. The guests are known to each other and the staff on a first-name or street-name basis. The soup kitchen is one of the few examples of a "hassle-free" or "problem-free" service in our society (Rousseau, 1981). The people, or "guests" as they are called in the soup kitchen nomenclature, know that the soup kitchen offers shelter for the morning and a hot meal at noon, yet there are no forms to fill out, no eligibility requirements to meet, no demands to "reform," "gain insight," or change.

The Soup Kitchen as an Urban Culture

The goal of this study is to describe the main features of the culture that emerges from the daily coming together of the guests in the dining room of the soup kitchen. Anthropology in particular has been concerned with the description and analysis of culture, or the ways in which people view their world, define reality, and organize their behavior (Spradley 1970). A useful characterization of culture is provided by Ward Goodenough, who states: "A society's culture consists of whatever it is one has to know or believe in order to operate in a manner acceptable to its members." (Goodenough 1957: 167). In working within modern, pluralistic societies, the term *subculture* is often used, recognizing that individuals also share the attributes of the dominant North American culture, as well as that of their own group. I will continue the tradition of many urban anthropologists (see, for example, Spradley 1970) and refer to the patterns of behavior in the soup kitchen dining room as a culture.

The culture of the soup kitchen is created as guests interact within the confines of the dining room, in what Anthony F. C. Wallace (1970: 26) calls *repetitive patterns of reciprocal interaction.* These patterns are created in part by the guests and in part by the staff, who enact the numerous rituals of daily soup kitchen life, including making coffee, serving doughnuts, announcing the menu, serving the meal, and socializing within the dining room. New guests are enculturated and learn proper soup kitchen behavior as they sit and observe the daily rituals of passing time and eating in the dining room. The soup kitchen culture then becomes one of the many cultures of an individual's repertoire.

Review of Works in Urban Anthropology

When anthropologists and other social scientists have entered the world of the poor in our society, they have often made discoveries and presented descriptions that have challenged stereotypes and had important social policy implications. One of the earliest examples of an in-depth study of people outside the mainstream of society was William Foote Whyte's classic *Street Corner Society* (1943). Whyte was able to form in-depth relationships with members of a group of young Italians in a street corner gang of an eastern city in the 1930s. Unlike earlier writers who characterized this type of community as "disorganized," he found a high degree of organization and activity. His personal relationships with the people moved Whyte and his readership beyond facile descriptions of them as clients of social agencies or criminals in the court system, to see them as individuals who had been inventive in their struggles for survival.

In the 1960s Elliot Liebow focused on the world of black men in a lower-class ghetto. Previous research had portrayed the black male as "absent" from community life. Liebow was able to chart the day-to-day life of the group of men he found at "Tally's Corner" (1967). He challenged the popular stereotype of the black male as being unmotivated to work, and in detail unearthed the realities of employment and unemployment for men in the black ghetto.

In a different vein, James Spradley (*You Owe Yourself a Drunk*, 1970) presented the cultural scene of the homeless men of Seattle's skid row, a group that is either avoided or stereotyped by the rest of society. Spradley referred to the men as urban nomads and tried to understand the insider's point of view. This cultural description made more comprehensible the "revolving-door" relationship that men charged with public drunkenness had with the jails and treatment centers to which they were sent. More recently, Ellen Baxter and Kim Hopper in *Private Lives/Public Spaces* (1981) directed attention to the contemporary homeless people of urban areas. Contrary to the belief that the homeless do not want shelter, they found that the men and women they came to know on the streets would indeed accept shelter if it was safe and offered with dignity. The Baxter and Hopper report is now frequently cited in discussions of homelessness.

The soup kitchen can be viewed as a social center and so has a similar role in the lives of the guests as did the Jewish Community

Center described in the work of Barbara Myerhoff in *Number Our Days* (1978). Myerhoff demonstrated the importance of the Jewish Community Center in the lives of elderly men and women. Her study viewed the Center through the eyes of its members, for whom it had become a surrogate family and surrogate village. In the Center the elderly tried to re-create the memories of their lives in the *shtetls* and ghettos of eastern Europe of almost a century ago. So too, I hypothesize that the present-day soup kitchen is a temporary surrogate family and community for a segment of the poor in a small city in New England.

Perhaps the most controversial work arising out of contemporary urban anthropology is that of Oscar Lewis and his characterizations of the "culture of poverty" (1966). Lewis attempted to generalize about people living in poverty, using his studies in urban Mexico, Puerto Rico, and New York as a base. He tried to explain what he saw as pervasive feelings of helplessness, pessimism, and despair. He hypothesized that the general tendency of the poor, especially those in industrialized, capitalistic nations, is to develop a particular set of cultural attributes as an adaptation to their lack of money, their high rates of unemployment, and their crowded and generally inhospitable living conditions. These characteristics then became self-defeating and self-perpetuating. He described the major characteristics of this "culture of poverty" as "the lack of effective participation and integration of the poor in the major institutions of the larger society . . . a minimum of organization beyond the level of the nuclear and extended family . . . an absence of childhood as a specially prolonged and protected stage in the life cycle . . . a strong feeling of marginality, of helplessness, of dependence and of inferiority" (Lewis 1966: 51–53).

The problem came about when the poor were seen to have family instability, a lack of effective participation in society's major institutions, and a sense of helplessness *because* of culturally transmitted values, rather than because of the economic and social processes of the larger social system. This focus on the "culture of poverty" implied that the burden of doing something about poverty was on the poor themselves, absolving the rest of society from considering the general economic and social system as a basic cause of poverty. The culture-of-poverty concept also tended to gloss over many of the variations that exist among low-income families. The soup kitchen may be seen as one culture within poverty that in fact is not self-defeating, but is a positive adaptation that cushions some of the harsh realities of life for its guests.

The majority of the guests of the soup kitchen are unemployed and are victims of what Daniel Bell (1973) has called the postindustrial society, in which technical and interpersonal skills have replaced willingness to work as the key to success in employment. In the postindustrial society, there is an illusion of advancement based solely on merit (meritocracy), so that poor people are made to internalize their "failures" in the competitive economic world. Many of the soup kitchen diners *never* had the chance to compete educationally, economically, or socially with the larger society. Cut off from the social life of school or work (and, for many, of family), the soup kitchen becomes a temporary, alternative way to fill their days without the success of employment, school, or money.

The soup kitchen diner may be seen as a member of a stratum of society that has been called the *underclass*—a word that Gunnar Myrdal introduced to the English-speaking world in the 1960s as a translation of the Swedish *underklasse* (Lawrence 1986; Myrdal 1962: 34). The *underclass* refers to people who are increasingly isolated from the rest of society, and who lack the education, employment experience, and literacy skills essential for upward mobility. What makes the underclass distinct from other low-income people is the *permanence* of their situation and their separation from others. The term *underclass* is a particularly useful one in that it transcends the traditional categories of welfare mothers, deinstitutionalized mentally ill, long-term unemployed, and inner-city minority youth that are used to describe groups in poverty in America. The term also distinguishes the contemporary poor from the poor of an earlier era who had the protection of a strong family (Auletta 1982). There is in addition a group of *new underclass*. This is the group of downwardly mobile people whose parents were members of the working class (Loewenstein 1985: 35–48). This new underclass has come about in large part because of the shift of the economy away from the predominance of low-skilled jobs to an increasing concentration on technical skills and communications fluency in the work force.

The site of the Tabernacle Soup Kitchen gives us an opportunity to see the underclass in a small urban area. Middle City is a former textile center in New England. Its population of 20,000 identifies it as an "urban locality" in the words of the U.S. Census for 1980. Middle City may be viewed as a small-scale metropolitan area, with all of the problems of crime, unemployment, poor housing, and unequal access to education and social and health services, though it contrasts sharply with some aspects of big city metropolitan conditions. Although Middle City is culturally diverse it has a very small black population. The diners of the Tabernacle Soup Kitchen add to our understanding of the composition of the underclass.

Cultural Themes of the Soup Kitchen

Soup kitchens serve an overt nutritional function for their guests. Beyond that are the important latent *social* functions they serve. In an effort to explore the various levels of meaning of the social life of the soup kitchen, I have identified three related but distinguishable themes that permeate the social interactions of the guests in the soup kitchen. These themes, which will be explored in depth in the chapters that follow, are sociability, acceptance, and the opportunity for some to become a part of a social network.

Sociability

For the group of people who are its guests, the soup kitchen provides an important focal point for the development of social contact and human interaction to meet basic needs of sociability. This general desire for human contacts, as distinguished from longer-term relationships, has been conceptualized by Georg Simmel (Wolff 1950) as "sociability." Sociologist Regina Kenen, in paraphrasing Simmel, defines sociability as "interaction that exists for its own sake, that is spoiled if its content grows significant or its emotional impact too strong, and that is separated from interaction solely geared to providing or receiving information. . . . The "sociability drive" is imperative for social life to flower and because even though sociability is not the equivalent or substitute for community, it may promote a feeling of community even when this is lacking" (Kenen 1982: 163).

The search for human interaction and sociability that occurs in the soup kitchen has recently been documented in other contemporary urban settings such as the neighborhood laundromat (Kenen 1982), and the secondhand clothing store (Wiseman 1979), and among groups of former and current drug addicts who loiter around methadone-maintenance clinics (Goldsmith et al. 1985). The soup kitchen, then, can be viewed as creating a modified, ephemeral, and temporary community, where feelings of connectedness with others can be expressed, however tentatively and guardedly. That is, a certain minimal level of social interaction is achieved, without strong ties or deep involvement. For some, this sociability can lead to the development of a more permanent and involved social-support network.

The soup kitchen contains some of the key elements that environmental psychologists have identified as being conducive to strangers approaching each other (Mehrabian and Russell 1975). This tendency to approach strangers, or to affiliate, can be identified when people previously unknown to each other have eye contact, smile, nod, greet one another, and begin a conversation. These beginnings of sociability can be seen occurring repeatedly in the soup kitchen setting. Moreover, at least two of the environmental attributes that Mehrabian and Russell identify as leading to affiliation—pleasure and "arousal"—appear to exist in the soup kitchen for the diners. The soup kitchen can be seen as a pleasant setting, in contrast to the single rooms and cramped apartments of most of the guests. The availability of doughnuts, coffee, bathrooms, and the permission to smoke, all lead to positive social feelings among the guests. The arousal factor is the anticipation of the meal to be served. It is interesting to note that, as soon as the meal is served and the guests have eaten, everyone quickly departs, not often stopping to chat and socialize at the exits. It is as though the soup kitchen has been defined by the meal, and that once the meal is over, the spell is broken.

In many ways, a soup kitchen is ideally suited to creating an ephemeral sense of community. The highlight of the day in the Tabernacle Soup Kitchen is the hot noontime meal, and food and companionship are intimately related. In their recent work on the anthropology of food and eating, Farb and Armelagos (1980) point out that the very word *companion* derives from French and Latin "one who eats bread [pain] with [com] others." People who eat together have a relationship with each other from the act of eating. The foods people eat, and the patterns of who eats with whom, capture some of the most important aspects of any society. Food and eating, then, are symbolic of the social position and social relationships of the individual. Perhaps it is symbolic of the rest of a person's life that the food of the soup kitchen is the leftovers of the rest of society, and that the food is eaten in the company of a temporary community of strangers.

Acceptance

The tendency to sociability in the soup kitchen is enhanced by a general atmosphere of acceptance of a great variety of behavior that would be seen as "deviant" in other settings. Although many of the guests have visible physical, mental, and social handicaps, these features are rarely noted or commented on by staff or other guests. There are no interviews held to assign diagnostic labels, as routinely occurs in health-care settings, for example. One never hears soup kitchen staff say "that alcoholic over there" or "the psychotic at that table." There are no case conferences held, and people are not treated as specimens or cases of some disease entity or other. This lack of labeling and categorizing, so unusual in contemporary America, has been called *deprofessionalism* (Scheper-Hughes 1983). The word *deprofessionalism* connotes a conscious omission of professionalism. The atmosphere of peaceful coexistence of a variety of "deviant" behaviors and conditions has also been seen as *benevolent anarchy* (Scheper-Hughes 1983). Anarchy reigns in the soup kitchen because there is little effort to impose a structure on the guests. It is benevolent, since the lack of structure is meant to convey a respect for the guests as adults who do not need to be infantilized by the rules and labels found in welfare offices and other agencies that serve the poor. The two rules that exist in the Tabernacle Soup Kitchen—no drinking alcohol or using drugs in the soup kitchen (though people may enter drunk or high), and no fighting—both seek to insure that the atmosphere of the soup kitchen is a safe one, and that the "anarchy" remains benevolent.

The deprofessionalized ambiance of acceptance brings to mind the original meanings of the words *sanctuary* and *asylum*, both signifying a place of refuge and protection from the outside world. The soup kitchen is indeed a temporary sanctuary and asylum for those outside the flow of life of the majority of the United States population. It is perhaps no accident that the common usage of the word *sanctuary* is religious, and the common usage of the word *asylum* connotes a place of refuge for the mentally ill. As further chapters will demonstrate, the soup kitchen is tied to concepts of religiosity and is a type of community setting (a temporary asylum) for many who have severe psychiatric problems.

Social Networks

The atmosphere of sociability and acceptance enables at least some of the guests to begin to affiliate in fairly consistent, predictable ways, forming social networks with each other. These networks are most dramatically indicated by the groupings around tables at which the guests regularly sit.

Social networks may be defined as a "set of linkages among a defined set of persons" (J. Mitchell 1969: 2). The term is related to but not identical with the concept of social support, which is the subjective evaluation of the social network in terms of benefits received by the individuals (Schaefer, Coyne, and Lazarus 1981: 381–406). These benefits, or support, may take the form of tangible, emotional, or informational help received from members of the social network.

The study of social networks became important as anthropology moved from the study of traditional, tribal cultures, where kinship relationships dominated people's behaviors, to urban settings where kinship ties hold a less central place (Wolfe 1978). The social network approach to the study of community was pioneered by John Barnes (1954), in his study of a fishing village in Norway, and Elizabeth Bott (1957), in her study of families in London.

The concepts of social network and social support have received a great deal of attention in the recent social science literature (Mitchell and Trickett 1980: 27–44) because of the strong association believed to exist between both concepts and physical and mental well-being. The soup kitchen is an important natural setting in which to study the emergence of social networks and social support. If indeed the dining room is a place in which networking and support flourish, this discovery may point to a previously untapped resource for self-help within a segment of the poor.

Conclusion

Soup kitchens have not been, to date, the subject of long-term, in-depth ethnographic study, despite their pervasiveness in American society. This research will continue the anthropological tradition of exploration and analysis of cultural patterns in economically and socially marginal populations. The study examines the meaning of the soup kitchen in the lives of the guests and the place of the soup kitchen in contemporary society. It utilizes a qualitative and quantitative methodology that is consonant with the nonthreatening ambiance of the setting. This research suggests that in many ways the soup kitchen is ideally suited to meeting some of the social needs of America's underclass, and that the soup kitchen setting has the potential for giving the more traditional health and social service providers a *model* of service that is congruent with the needs of this group of people. The research also gives us an opportunity to view how diverse groups of poor people interact when they regularly meet within the closed space of a dining room. The soup kitchen, therefore, represents a rather unique opportunity to study emergent patterns of social interaction and communication among individuals with widely diverse backgrounds in terms of age, sex, parenthood, ethnicity, and mental and physical states of health and illness.

For George Smith, the Tabernacle Soup Kitchen became the site of life's ultimate rite of passage, just as in life it had become the center of his social existence. For another hundred people who are without work, are physically or mentally ill, live in unfriendly or dangerous surroundings, and exist on the meager incomes of welfare programs, the soup kitchen creates a culture in which the desire for sociability, acceptance, and social support may be at least fleetingly realized.

2

A Historical Perspective

Soup kitchens have moved from the popular image of storefront dining rooms with steaming vats, serving an elderly, alcoholic population, to a pervasive movement throughout the United States, serving a diverse group of men, women, and children. There now appear to be more soup kitchens in the United States than there have been at any time since the Great Depression.

Before turning to an examination of the Tabernacle Soup Kitchen, it is instructive to ask: To what is this renaissance attributable? In order to begin to answer the question, it is necessary to examine both historical and current data documenting the existence of soup kitchens. Unfortunately, this task is a difficult one, in part because the term *soup kitchen* is not used in classifying social science literature. Neither is the term necessarily utilized by agencies concerned with services to the poor. For example, although the Salvation Army provides between 10 and 12 million meals annually to people in feeding stations and temporary housing, it does not officially recognize the term *soup kitchen* as a separate category of service (personal communication, Lieutenant Colonel Beatrice Combs, 1985).

Although soup kitchens rarely appear in the professional social science literature, they are frequently cited in the popular press. They are often pointed to as barometers of poverty in America, as illustrated here:

The commission found most of the poor concentrated in three areas, where they were isolated from the rest of the city. . . . Last winter the soup kitchens in all three neighborhoods began serving double shifts of the mid-day meal because of the growing crowds (*New York Times* 1983: 22).

A contemporary definition of soup kitchens is offered in the report *American Hunger Crisis* (Harvard University 1984). Soup kitchens are

places where a meal, usually lunch or dinner, is served on a regular basis (daily or weekly). Kitchens are typically located in churches, shelters for the homeless, or community centers. They are staffed by volunteers who plan, prepare, and serve a full meal at little or no cost to as many as several hundred people. Meals range from soup or a sandwich and beverage to a full-course hot dinner (Harvard University 1984: Glossary).

Historical References to Soup Kitchens

One of the first references to soup kitchens appears to be in discussions of the potato famine of Ireland in the nineteenth century. The Soup Kitchen Act of 1847 provided that sites be established for mass feeding the starving population (Aykroyd 1975). According to the records of the time, the beneficiaries were humiliated, and many suffered ill effects from the watery soup. In the book *The Conquest of Famine*, Aykroyd assesses the success of the soup kitchens:

Well-meaning people honestly thought that a sure way of relieving the famine had been found. But unfortunately little was known in the mid-nineteenth century about food values and human nutritional requirements. "Soup" means hot water in which heterogeneous ingredients have been boiled, but it is mostly hot water. There were many different recipes for the soup doled out to the starving, including some devised by the famous French chef, Alexis Soyer, then employed in London, who set up a demonstra-

tion kitchen in Dublin. Among the ingredients were oxheads
(without the tongues), maize, carrots, turnips, cabbages, onions,
peas, leeks and other things. A bowl of such soup was no doubt
warm and comforting, but it probably provided less than 200
calories to people needing up to 3000 calories daily. Famine oede-
ma or dropsy . . . became widespread in 1847, and it is possible
that the soup, by a "water-logging" effect, contributed to its
occurrence. (Aykroyd 1975: 36)

In the United States, soup kitchens were pervasive in the 1930s
as an attempt to feed the 25 percent of the work force that was
unemployed (Axinn and Levin 1975). In a personal communication
with me, one recipient of food at a Depression soup kitchen remi-
nisces about his experiences.

I am fascinated by your request of recollections of social inter-
action of diners in soup kitchens; I assume that you have in mind
the venerable and socially useful institution during the Great
Depression.
I have lived through that period as a resident of New York City
and although I doubt that my recollection is of much use to you,
I feel introspective and retrospective pleasure in my memories
by reliving them in this brief account to you.
I "dined" several times in a soup kitchen endowed by Bernard
McFadden and I still carry a surge of gratitude to that man. . . .
McFadden's dining establishment was located in mid-town
Manhattan, on the west side of either 32 or 33 street, and he
offered nourishing food at the price of 1 cent per serving. For 5
cents or less one could have a quite satisfactory meal, without
any hint of charity, because money was demanded and paid. As
I recall, there were long lines of "diners" but I don't recall any
social interaction between them and, strange to say, I cannot
remember any women among them. We all seemed to be pretty
dull and sullen, and food was more important than any other
subject. I am speaking of the very harsh winter of 32–33, with
much snow and bitter cold. . . . Finally I found work . . . as a

dishwasher in a newly established restaurant for $12.00 a week plus two meals a day—those were days of 12 hours each for six consecutive days—but it gave me the chance of looking for other more lucrative opportunities. These finally arrived in August 1934, mostly as the result of the "New Deal" Administration of President Franklin D. Roosevelt. . . . It may interest you to know that those hard and difficult days of soup kitchens have made me a life-long and unquestioning Democrat.

I'd be happy to know that these personal memories of a survivor may be of use to a young person. (Personal communication from a New Jersey man, May, 1985)

The Contemporary Soup Kitchen Movement

I am suggesting that soup kitchens have again become a fact of North American life because of four major developments that have affected poverty and society's response to it. Those developments are chronic unemployment and the development of an underclass; the deinstitutionalization of the mentally ill; the shrinkage of the federal "safety net" programs; and the heightened awareness of the hungry and homeless in the midst of an otherwise affluent society.

Development of an Underclass

Poverty in the United States has changed its character, both in terms of the composition of the group on the bottom rung of society, and in its relative permanence and separation from the rest of society. This calcification of the poor into a caste-like stratum is frequently referred to as the development of an *underclass*.

Most social scientists who write about poverty agree that there has been an actual decline in the proportion of poor in America in the last twenty years. However, there has been a shift in who is poor. For example, in 1959 22.4 percent of the population lived below the threshold of poverty, whereas in 1979 11.6 percent lived in poverty (Kammerman 1982). Most of the improvement in the

poverty rates occurred before 1972, particularly in the rural south, and was due to an improvement and expansion of income transfer programs (welfare) and social insurance (e.g., Social Security) programs. However, the rate of poverty in northern cities has remained the same or worsened since 1959 (Blaustein 1982).

The poverty rates are drawn from a measure of absolute poverty developed by the Social Security Administration in 1965. The formula used to establish the poverty threshold is generally arrived at by estimating the market cost of the Economy Food Plan of the Department of Agriculture, multiplied by three (Preston 1984). However, the Economy Food Plan was never meant to be more than an emergency plan for a family. The conservative nature of the federal measure of poverty becomes clear when one realizes that in 1980 the poverty threshold for a family of four was $7,450.

Beyond the numbers of people in poverty, it is clear that there has been a major shift in the categories in poverty. The movement has been from the elderly and two-parent wage-earner households of the 1950s to a concentration of poverty within households of women and children (78 percent of the poor) and members of ethnic minorities today (Kammerman 1980). In addition, of those who live alone and are unemployed, 48 percent are poor (Levitan 1978).

Almost all the guests of the Tabernacle Soup Kitchen are unemployed, although they are within the ages of eighteen to sixty-five that are usually associated with work force participation. Most are a part of the *chronically* unemployed, which is technically defined as those who are out of work for twenty-seven or more weeks (Sherraden 1985). The rest are members of the group of *discouraged workers*, the term used by the Department of Labor for those people who are not registered for work. The discouraged workers are not usually counted in the national unemployment statistics. The category may include a significant number of people, and, without them, the unemployment rate can be seriously distorted. For example, in the recession of 1975, the official unemployment rate was 8.8, whereas a conservative estimate that included the discouraged worker would have increased it to 12 percent (Sherman 1976).

The research on the long-term effects of unemployment points to an increase in the incidence of clinical depression, the loss of self-esteem and self-worth, and an increased propensity toward physical illness (Keefe 1984). The lack of employment, and subsequent lack of money, also restricts the consumption of goods and services. This lack of ability to participate in after-work-hours consumerism can be seen as whittling away at individual self-worth, making reentry into the job market even more difficult. This in turn solidifies the individual's sense of marginality and alienation from the mainstream. When the unemployed are young (less than forty years old), as is true of the majority of guests of the soup kitchen, the situation becomes even more urgent, since they are faced with a life filled with boredom and despair.

Deinstitutionalization

Along with the rise in the number of permanently unemployed is a rise in the numbers of mentally ill on the streets. This phenomenon is usually referred to under the rubric *deinstitutionalization*. On the one hand, the term refers to the actual emptying out of large state mental hospitals, from a count of 559,000 inpatients in 1955 to approximately 132,000 in 1983 (Redick and Witkin 1983). Deinstitutionalization also refers to those policies which divert back to the streets people who would have been committed to a state psychiatric hospital two or three decades ago, and to policies which have made psychiatric hospitalizations relatively short for those who are admitted (Bachrach 1984). The services in the community for the mentally ill, which were supposed to expand in conjunction with deinstitutionalization, have been almost totally inadequate or nonexistent. Many of the mentally ill have become homeless, inmates of jails and prisons, or drifters from one community to the next (Lamb 1984).

As later chapters will indicate, many of the guests of the Tabernacle Soup Kitchen have significant mental health problems. They come to the soup kitchen for its warmth and its food, and for a place to spend some hours in the company of others, with no demands made. One interesting indication of the problem of where the mentally ill may spend their day is the attendance recently of 350 librarians at a workshop on ways to deal with the mentally disturbed library patron (Jaynes 1981). Along with soup kitchen, libraries have become one way the mentally ill on the streets pass the hours in relative warmth and safety.

Shrinking of Federal Spending on the Poor

It has been more than twenty years since the initial federal investments of money in the Great Society programs directed toward the amelioration of poverty, and there has been a growing cynicism about the benefits of the efforts to date. Since the first Reagan administration, there have been significant reductions in the extent of the "safety net" programs of the federal government. For example, in the area of nutrition programs, there has been a reduction amounting to $12.2 billion during the years 1982–1985 (Harvard University 1984). A recent hunger study directed by the Harvard School of Public Health estimates that there are now 20 million Americans who suffer from hunger, out of the 35.3 million Americans who live under the federal definition of poverty (Harvard University 1985). The numbers of people in poverty include a substantial proportion of children, for whom the effects of hunger are cumulative and affect educational, social, and future economic status. The 35 million in poverty also include 15 million people who, for a variety of reasons, are not receiving food stamps, the largest federal food program (Harvard University 1985).

The shrinkage in federal spending has occurred with no lessening of the numbers of people in poverty. In fact, there has been an increase from 11 percent in 1979, to 14 percent in 1982 (Dukert 1983). In 1986 the United States Conference on Mayors reported an increase in the cases of hunger and homelessness in twenty-five cities, including Puerto Rico (*New York Times* January 21, 1986).

Heightened Awareness of Hunger and Homelessness

For many Americans, the reports of starving children and elderly people freezing to death on the streets are a shocking contrast to the affluence of the rest of society. Many religious and voluntary groups are responding in direct aid to the hungry and homeless. Some analysts have suggested that this involvement is part of a movement to see poverty issues in concrete terms of food and shelter, avoiding the larger, underlying issues of inequality in America (Stern 1984). Religious groups are often the vehicle for the expression of concern for the most destitute of society. In fact, soup kitchens are often directly related to the religious community. In Connecticut, for example, approximately 80 percent of the soup kitchens are affiliated with Christian churches (estimate of Mark Patton, Connecticut Food Bank, personal communication, 1986).

In many ways, soup kitchens and shelters embody aspects of *charity*, a concept that was popular in an earlier era. Historically, charity has implied inequality between giver and receiver. In the United States, charity was the response to unmet survival needs until the Great Depression of the 1930s made this an inadequate response.

On the other hand, soup kitchens may be thought of as being in the vanguard of bringing services to people in a nonbureaucratic, "paperless," hassle-free form. One recent report in the *New York Times* Business section (Peters 1985) reported on the trend for business corporations to move toward "paperless organization" in an attempt to cut down needless, demoralizing middle layers of management that severely limit the contact of top decisionmakers with the rank-and-file workers. The analogy with soup kitchens is that in eliminating paperwork, charts, folders, etc., there is a direct link between soup kitchen workers and guests, and the operation is more humanized.

Conclusion

Soup kitchens have resurfaced on the American scene as individual citizens have become aware of the destitute who are painfully visible on the streets. Soup kitchens appear to have developed as a response to the widely publicized problems of chronic unemployment and the deinstitutionalization of the 1970s and 1980s. Feeding the hungry appears to express the need of many Americans to offer nourishment to the poor in a direct, nonbureaucratic manner. This nonprofessionalized response to poverty, as we shall see in subsequent chapters, has some interesting and beneficial consequences for the poor themselves, which go well beyond a hot noontime meal.

3

The Tabernacle Soup Kitchen

The Tabernacle Soup Kitchen in Middle City is one of forty soup kitchens in a northeastern state. It is located in the basement of Saint Mary's Church, and serves a hot noontime meal, six days a week. Saint Mary's Church is Protestant in denomination and has a congregation of approximately 250 members. The parishioners are heterogeneous in economic and educational status, with a fairly large proportion coming from two nearby university communities. The soup kitchen was established in 1981, when the City Ministry committee of the church decided that the number of poor and hungry in Middle City had grown to alarming proportions. For five years preceding the establishment of the soup kitchen, Saint Mary's City Ministry had provided free suppers to the city's poor on Thursday evenings. The free suppers were a way for the church to provide a concrete service to the poor. It was an opportunity for Saint Mary's parishioners to have direct association with a portion of the population with whom they would have little contact in their daily lives.

Saint Mary's Church conceives of the soup kitchen as a part of its ministry to the poor. On the first page of the City Ministry brochure, under the heading *Our Call—Our Commitment* the ministry is described as follows:

St. Mary's lies in the heart of the city, and the city lies in the heart of St. Mary's. The city's problems are our problems: urban

23

poverty, a large deinstitutionalized population, the closing of local industry, an unemployment rate above the national average. These problems and our commitment are the foundation of our call to ministry.

Another of the City Ministry's newsletters expressed the work of the parishioners with the poor as "living the gospel."

Since 1981 the Tabernacle Soup Kitchen has been feeding an average of 80 to 100 persons six days a week. It is administered by the City Ministry committee, which also sponsors a food pantry and an emergency fuel fund. The minister who directed the initial effort that created the Tabernacle Soup Kitchen was the Reverend Smith, a dynamic man, who, one year after the beginnings of the soup kitchen, left the area for a much larger community. In the next three years, Saint Mary's saw one new minister and two assistant ministers come and then leave the parish. For one full year Saint Mary's was without a spiritual director, yet the soup kitchen program continued without interruption. This suggests that the soup kitchen has a life of its own and is not dependent on a particular minister.

Not all of Saint Mary's 250 members are enthusiastic supporters of the soup kitchen. Some individuals complain about the physical deterioration of the church caused by extensive use. The disagreements are symbolized by discussions concerning the sign hanging outside the church announcing the soup kitchen's existence. During the first two years there were complaints about the unsightliness of the large hand-drawn sign, and it was replaced by a smaller, more discreet, professionally lettered sign. The discussions about the sign seem to be a way for the church members to express their feelings about the soup kitchen guests (many of whom are as "unsightly" as the initial sign), without confronting the issue of the church's ministry to the poor.

Saint Mary's is a gray stone Gothic-type building one block from the downtown area of the city. In order to enter the soup kitchen, one must descend a set of stairs leading to the church basement. A strong odor of cleaning materials, perspiration, and old food greets

one at the entrance. There is a rest room for women on the floor above the basement, and a men's room off the dining room. These bathrooms are an important convenience in the life of the soup kitchen, where the guests may spend three and four hours at a time.

The dining room is large, open, and dimly lit, and contains thirty old Formica-topped tables dispersed throughout the room. In one corner there is a blackened piece of rug, several high chairs, and a crib. This is the children's corner, and often young mothers and their children take the tables nearest the rug area. During the summers of 1983, 1984, and 1985 there were children's programs and preschool activities centered in this area. In the middle of the ceiling of the dining room is an air purifier, which was anonymously donated to deal with the abundant smoke that accumulates from the cigarettes of the guests.

At the opposite end of the room from the children's corner is a countertop which holds a fifty-cup coffeepot. During the mornings, day-old doughnuts are placed near the pot along with reconstituted dried milk. There is also a coffeepot filled with cold water for the children. Occasionally, sliced fruit such as apples or oranges is served. The coffeepot area is the center of much activity from 9 A.M., when the soup kitchen opens, until 12 noon, by which time the coffee and doughnuts have disappeared.

In the back of the dining room is a large, institutional-looking kitchen which contains a stove, aluminum sinks and countertops, two refrigerators, and cabinets used to store the plates and glasses. Off the kitchen are several large pantries. In a side room are two large freezers and several tables and chairs. This room is used as a dining room for the staff, volunteers, and *workfare* workers who have prepared the soup kitchen meal; they eat their dinner before serving the guests at 12:30. Beyond this room is an office used by the director and her assistants. The office is also piled high with cartons of United States Department of Agriculture surplus foods. During the Thanksgiving and Christmas seasons, peak times for soup kitchen donations, the office floor area is filled with cartons of food. There is often the odor of old apples and other fruits and vegetables in these rooms off the kitchen, since many people donate leftover produce from their gardens and orchards. The abundant space of Saint Mary's recalls an earlier time in the church's history when parish members were more numerous and churches played a more central role in the social life of their members.

From 1981 to 1983 the kitchen was directed by Jean, a college-educated woman in her midtwenties. She was a widow with a young child. Jean had met Father Smith when she was a social worker for the state. She told me that she had been looking for a way to relate to people in a more direct way, and she was very enthusiastic about the soup kitchen and her newly found relationship with Christianity. After two years Jean left to return to graduate school and was replaced by Christine, who has been the director ever since. Christine is a woman in her middle thirties, who has a master's degree in a human service field. Under Christine's direction, the soup kitchen became a smoothly running, orderly operation, in contrast with the rather frantic quality of its first two years. Christine also takes a greater interest in nutrition and has tried to educate herself and her kitchen workers about ways to maximize the nutritional content of the daily meal. Like Jean, Christine sees her work in the soup kitchen as closely tied to her relationship to Christianity.

During the eight months between June, 1983, and January, 1984, the soup kitchen staff included a registered nurse for twenty hours a week. The nurse provided health education, first aid, and information and referral for the guests. When the nurse, Rachel, left, the City Ministry committee decided not to replace her. In January, 1985, they hired a half-time assistant director for the soup kitchen. Fran, the assistant director, supervises the kitchen crew, interacts with the guests, and oversees on Saturdays. In addition to this paid staff, there was a part-time recreation director during the summers of 1983 through 1987, who directed the program of activities for children of the guests during the summer mornings. For most of the soup kitchen's history, the paid staff has included a director and one other staffperson, in the form of a nurse, a recreation director, or an assistant.

The kitchen crew is staffed by people on the *workfare* program and by community volunteers. Workfare is an adjunct to the general assistance program (commonly referred to as town welfare) of Middle City. The program requires that people receiving town welfare work for fifteen or twenty hours a week in public service jobs, in order to "pay back" their welfare allotment. If they complete their assigned hours, they receive an additional $10 of "incentive pay." The workfare sites are public service and maintenance jobs of city government and nonprofit agencies. The fifteen Tabernacle Soup Kitchen workfare workers are assigned to maintenance and food preparation jobs for four or five days a week. They are most often people who were guests of the soup kitchen before their workfare assignment there, and they continue to be guests on their days off. Most of the guests who become workfare workers in the soup kitchen seem to perceive it as a step up from guest status. They are allowed access to the kitchen, Christine's office, and the kitchen telephone. They eat in a smaller, separate dining area before the noontime meal, so that they can help with the serving. Recently, the soup kitchen has become a site for the Job Training Partnership Act, so the workfare crew can receive more formal instruction in kitchen work, in order that they may eventually find employment in the competitive job market.

There is also a cadre of fifteen or twenty community volunteers, most of whom are retired men and women who volunteer one or two days of work in the soup kitchen. Many are affiliated with area churches (including Saint Mary's) and view this work as part of their religious commitment. Among the volunteers are several women in their sixties who have reared large families and appear to be proud of their cooking and baking skills. One man is a retired school cafeteria cook who regularly wears his professional chef's hat in the kitchen. On Saturdays a community church or organization prepares and serves the meal. It appears that the Protestant and Catholic church groups are well represented in the volunteer corps, whereas there is very little participation by the Hispanic and Jewish groups. There appears to be little outreach on the part of the soup kitchen staff to recruit members of the Hispanic group, despite the fact that between 15 and 30 percent of the guests are Hispanic. The Jewish community perceives the soup kitchen as a part of a proselytizing Christian *ministry*. In fact, I did not observe overt proselytizing there, although occasionally guests involved in some of the fundamentalist Protestant groups tried to interest other guests in Bible study or in going to their church services.

The menus for the soup kitchen are decided on each day by Christine, based on the availability of donated and purchased food. For the past year, a registered dietician has volunteered consultation to the director on the nutritional needs of the guests, many of whom rely on the soup kitchen for their one full hot meal of the day. On most days, the soup kitchen meal includes foods from the protein, bread, milk, and vegetable food groups. Fruits are served whenever they are donated, which is irregularly.

The food for the Tabernacle Soup Kitchen is obtained from a variety of sources. Most of the donated food is canned, packaged goods, and fresh produce from individuals in the community. Some of the food comes from commercial sources, where old or unsold food would otherwise be thrown away. This recycling of food from commercial sources is known as *food salvage*. For example, a pastry shop fifteen miles away from the soup kitchen donates its day-old doughnuts to the kitchen. A church group in the community has taken on the task of transporting the doughnuts from the store to the soup kitchen daily. Another kind of donation comes from organizations that have had a social function the previous evening, and have leftover food. One morning when I was on the kitchen crew, a local group donated enough sausage and peppers to feed over a hundred people. This kind of donation makes meal planning almost impossible, but it does offer the soup kitchen guests some variety.

The soup kitchen also purchases foods from the State Bureau of Purchases in a neighboring city. These supplies include a variety of foods from cake flour to canned meats and vegetables, which are sold to the soup kitchen at 25 percent of the original price. There are also the government surplus foods—cheese, rice, butter, powdered milk, and flour. Food drives at Thanksgiving and Christmas supply the soup kitchen with a variety of canned and packaged goods, and in the summer, there is a steady supply of fresh vegetables. Most of the donated foods are usable, although the director uses her judgment in discarding foods of questionable quality. For example, unidentified foods that people wrap in plastic bags and donate to the soup kitchen in food drives are discarded. When Christine first arrived, she discovered a donated raccoon in the bottom of the freezer. Since she had no idea how long it had been there, she discarded it. She speaks of the importance of graciously accepting community donations, even those that may be discreetly disposed of later.

At approximately 12:20, before the dinner is served, Christine stands in front of the serving table, waiting for the group of approximately one hundred guests to be quiet. She then states the menu for the day and asks if there are any announcements. She often mentions something of interest to the guests, such as the registration for cheese and butter distribution at the Town Hall that day. She then asks if anyone would like to say the prayer before the meal. Sometimes a guest will stand up and say a prayer. Usually Christine says a short Christian prayer. She then asks a guest or a volunteer to pick a card from a small deck, and she reads the number, which corresponds to cards which have been placed on each table. The guests at the table whose card has been called then proceed to the serving line. In this way the table to be served first is randomly chosen each day. The rest of the cards are then chosen and read, until all of the guests have been served the meal.

The meal is served at 12:30 by community volunteers and some of the workfare workers, who say a word or two of greeting to each person. Recently, new serving tables were purchased with the money collected in memory of George, a regular soup kitchen guest who had died. A meal might consist of frankfurters cut up into small pieces, baked beans, a salad, bread, butter, and a dessert such as plain cake. There are at times five-ounce glasses of juice, and there is usually milk for the children and pregnant women, with some left over for a few other guests. There appears to be very little food wasted, based on my observations of what people throw away as they scrape their plates.

After about ten minutes, as the first guests are finishing their food, Christine announces the availability of seconds. Typically, there are second servings of vegetables and carbohydrate-rich foods. Usually all of the meal prepared for that day is eaten. Any leftovers are stored for another soup kitchen meal or are frozen in small quantities to be given to people who come to the *food pantry*, another feeding ministry of Saint Mary's Church.

By 1 P.M. the guests are through with their meal, and the workfare workers clean up the dining room. Unlike the rather leisurely and social morning time before the meal, there is no lingering afterwards. The workfare crew as well as the volunteers seem eager to leave, and the guests receive the message that the soup kitchen is over for the day.

Middle City is a community of 20,000 people that includes French Canadian, eastern Europeans, and Puerto Ricans (Regional Planning Agency of Middle City 1980). It was once a thriving industrial town, but many of the factories have closed, and the jobs that are now available require more training and education, including construction, communications, finance, health services, and teaching. The city is also the commercial and service center for a population of approximately 37,000 living in the surrounding rural communities.

Middle City is the sixth-poorest town in the state, with 13 percent of its population having an income below the federal poverty line, which in 1980 was $7,382 for a family of four. In 1980 the median income of the state was $20,078, in contrast to the median income for Middle City which was $14,353 (Regional Planning Agency). As in the national data, poverty in Middle City is found disproportionately among the female-headed households with children; Hispanic and nonwhite populations; and among people living alone (*Poverty in the Region* 1980). The major ethnic minority group in Middle City is Hispanic (most of whom are Puerto Rican). This group was reported to number approximately 1,600 (8 percent) in the city's 1980 Census data. It should be noted, however, that the Census data on the number of the Hispanic population in the United States is thought to be generally undercounted due to frequent migration and underreporting (Giachello et al. 1983). In Middle City this underreporting may be due in part to the tendency to report relatives as "just visiting" from Puerto Rico, when in fact this visit turns into a permanent stay. The Tabernacle Soup Kitchen population, like the poor of Middle City, is composed of single women with children, Hispanics, and people living alone.

Except for the area around Main Street, the poor of Middle City suffer from a peculiar kind of invisibility, despite the fact that they are almost one-seventh of the population. During the early 1970s, Middle City went through a redevelopment effort whose purpose and effect was to improve the appearance of the downtown area. In accomplishing this, five square blocks were torn down to make room for a cinema, parking lots, and a housing project for the elderly. The inhabitants of these streets, who were primarily low-income and included a significant Hispanic population, were moved from the area. Since the city has few apartments for low-income tenants, many were moved three miles outside of the city limits to Windy Heights, a privately owned, federally subsidized housing project. Until the past year, there was no public transportation from the Heights to the city. People who lived there were cut off from employment opportunities, shopping, and needed health and social services. The 1,500 to 2,000 tenants of Windy Heights are 80 percent Hispanic.

Most of the poor of Middle City live in the residential areas on or near Main Street. There are three small public (subsidized) housing projects near town. In addition, there is a single-room-occupancy (SRO) hotel (Hotel Paradise) and several SRO houses which are rented to single people living on town welfare. These rooms typically have no stove or refrigerator available, and the tenants must surreptitiously bring in hot plates if they want to have warm food in their rooms. These rooms do not usually require a security deposit and are often the only housing available to people receiving town welfare. Many of the guests of the Tabernacle Soup Kitchen live in these rooms.

Perhaps the most visible group of poor people in Middle City are the men who stand outside the Hotel Paradise all day and into much of the night. For them, both the sidewalk and the soup kitchen are their usual areas of daily living and socializing.

Middle City is served by two large umbrella human service agencies that serve a twenty-town area. One is the antipoverty community action agency which includes a Puerto Rican program, a storefront crisis intervention service, fuel assistance, and a shelter for families temporarily homeless, twenty miles outside of Middle City. The other agency, a community mental health center, includes victim assistance, child and adult psychotherapy, Hispanic services, a halfway house, supervised apartments for former psychiatric patients, advocacy for the chronically mentally ill, and drug and alcohol services. Middle City also has a youth services bureau and a halfway house for drug dependent young people. There is a 250-bed general hospital and a small psychiatric hospital. Town welfare (general assistance) is available at the Town Hall, and state welfare may be applied for in a city twenty miles away. There is very limited public transportation within Middle City.

Middle City is a quasi-urban community, which is considered the center for the health, service, and commercial needs of the surrounding rural community. Middle City can be seen as a typical small New England city that was once a mill town and has undergone great changes in recent decades, both in economy and ethnic composition.

Soup kitchens are often thought of as an urban phenomenon, and therefore it is perhaps surprising that a place like Middle City has one. Although Middle City is moderately well provided with human services, the soup kitchen serves a social need for a portion of the poor community that the more traditional health and service agencies do not serve. The soup kitchen provides a comfortable atmosphere for its guests, in which social relationships are able to form. It proved to be an ideal research setting for an enhanced understanding of the life of a population of poor people, in that it was possible to establish relationships with the guests over a period of time. The soup kitchen also provided an opportunity to study the impact of an institution not previously examined.

4

Field Study Methods

The soup kitchen is one of the few places in modern life where questions are not asked, folders and charts are not kept, and where there are no eligibility requirements. The challenge of field research within a soup kitchen is to develop methods for gathering information in a manner that is compatible with the nonthreatening, paperless, "no-questions-asked" spirit of the setting. The methods must be unobtrusive, must insure the privacy of the individual guests, and must be conducted in a manner that will not alienate any of the guests or potential guests and deter them from coming.

The major method utilized in the study of the Tabernacle Soup Kitchen was that of *ethnography*. An ethnography seeks to describe a culture and understand it from the native point of view (Spradley 1979). The ethnography utilizes both qualitative and quantitative research strategies in order to comprehend most fully the culture of the group.

In the ethnography of the Tabernacle Soup Kitchen the qualitative method of participant observation sought to understand and describe the meaning of the soup kitchen for its guests through four years of listening, observing, and participating in the daily life of the dining room. The quantitative method sought to document the important social, economic, and health characteristics of the guests through two systematic surveys. These two strategies parallel the *emic* and *etic* distinctions that have been useful in anthropology (Pelto and Pelto 1970). The emic methodology strives to obtain the insider's point of view and his interpretation of the meaning of events and relationships. As much as is possible, I have used the words of the guests to arrive at their world view of the meaning of the soup kitchen in their lives. The etic methodology seeks to understand the pattern of behavior in categories defined by the observer. The surveys conducted in the soup kitchen sought to discover patterns of the soup kitchen guests in regard to categories such as age, ethnicity, income, and health status.

The qualitative and quantitative methods enhanced each other. I began with participant observation, which led to the formulation of research questions, some of which could best be addressed through systematic interviews. The data then gathered through interviews needed the understanding that came with extensive participation within the dining room.

I participated in the Tabernacle Soup Kitchen from the early spring of 1983 through the spring of 1987. Throughout that period, I tried to talk with as many as possible of the eighty to one hundred guests who ate there daily, and I maintained in-depth relationships with approximately fifty guests. The soup kitchen is an ever-changing community, where approximately 65 percent of the guests change every three to six months. This meant that I attained at least face recognition and the casual acquaintance of several hundred guests over the course of the study.

As a part of the ethnography, I also taught three series of classes about community resources for those daily soup kitchen guests who were considered leaders or who were interested. The classes were conducted for five weeks in the spring of 1984, for six weeks in the fall of 1985, and for six weeks in the winter of 1987. The purpose of the classes was to give a group of regular soup kitchen guests information about community services that was relevant to themselves and the other guests. The people in the class, it was anticipated, would be indigenous leaders within the soup kitchen, and would then be able to disseminate the information in an effective manner. In the book *Number Our Days* (1978), Barbara Myerhoff described her class in Living History as her way of offering the Jewish Community Center something she was capable of giving. It also provided her, as the indigenous worker class did for me, a way of knowing people in more depth than casual conversations usually produce.

I first entered the soup kitchen on March 14, 1983. I had heard of the Tabernacle Soup Kitchen from some of my sociology students who talked about the many hours guests stayed in the dining room, and described the nonbureaucratic atmosphere. My first impression was that of a chaotic, smoke-filled dining room. It seemed as though all of the "street people" of Middle City were in one place at once. Babies were crying, people were talking loudly with each other. One table appeared to be occupied (in the sense of a military takeover) by big men with beards, metal chains hanging from their belts, and leather jackets with large silver studs protruding from their shoulders. I sat next to one heavily tattooed woman who appeared to be in her early twenties, who had had a baby two weeks earlier. The woman asked me, a total stranger to her, to feed her crying baby a bottle. I said I would, but as I began, I noticed that the nipple did not seem to be allowing any of the milk to come out. As I was explaining this to the young mother, a tall woman came over. She appeared to be in her forties, with bleached blond, frizzy hair. Without speaking a word, she saw what the problem was, took a large safety pin off her belt, and stuck the nipple with it in order to widen the opening. I was impressed with this very direct and immediate offer of help.

During the next four years, I began to see the soup kitchen as less chaotic. As I came to know the guests, I was impressed with its part in their survival strategy for life in often impoverished and difficult conditions. I came to see the dining room, which had at first appeared to me to be loud, dirty, and barren, as actually a pleasant and safe place to spend the morning hours of a long day.

Relationships with Guests

In gaining rapport with the guests, I followed what I came to regard as soup kitchen protocol. I would pour myself some coffee from the pot at the front of the dining room, ask a guest with an empty chair near him if I could sit down (in this way respecting the privatizing of public space that often occurs in public settings), and introduce myself. I would introduce myself by first name, as I noticed most of the guests did with each other, and explained that I was a professor at a nearby college, that some of my students had worked in the soup kitchen, and that I wanted to learn more about it. A conversation would usually ensue on topics such as the food at the Tabernacle Soup Kitchen, the employment picture in Middle City, or how long the person had lived in the area. Sometimes the guests would tell me their recent history, such as that they had just gotten out of the hospital or jail, and at other times this first contact would just establish our names. The Puerto Rican guests tended to be very friendly, in part because most had recently moved to Middle City from Puerto Rico or from other cities, and they were eager to make acquaintances. I consciously tried to vary the table at which I sat each day, in order to know as many of the guests as possible.

I found that the best time to get to know the guests was from 9:30 A.M. through the mealtime. During much of the period of the study I spent two mornings a week at the soup kitchen, occasionally visiting every day. During the summers of 1983, 1984, and 1986 I supervised college students who were directing a recreation program for the children of the guests.

Throughout the time of the study, I maintained contact with many of the guests who became my key informants. The following is a description of some who offered their time to teach me the meaning of the soup kitchen to them.

The Gamache Family

This was an extended family consisting of the mother, Marie, her three daughters, Joan, Sally, and Nicole, and the four children of Sally and the two children of Joan. Marie had custody of Steve, Sally's oldest child. Throughout the study, at least some members of the family were consistent soup kitchen guests, and I developed an especially close relationship with Marie and Joan, both of whom were members of the community counseling course. Joan and Sally and their children lived in one of the low-income housing projects, and Marie and Nicole lived in an apartment above a store on Main Street. After the period of time of the study, two-year-old Teddy, Sally's youngest child, was killed in a flash fire that spread through a friend's apartment where Teddy was staying for the morning.

Madeline

At the time I entered the soup kitchen, Madeline was one of the workfare kitchen crew who was friendly to me. She was a tall woman of twenty-five, with long black hair. Her face was often filled with pimples and cuts. She told me that she had recently been discharged from the state psychiatric facility, and that she had a child of three who was now in the custody of her sister in another state. She lived on town welfare in a room in a local rooming house that guests referred to as the "thieves' den." Madeline became louder and louder as the months wore on. I would see her in the street weaving in and out of traffic. She lost her position on workfare, and by the end of the fall of 1984, she had been recommitted to the psychiatric facility. Approximately six months after that, I resumed my contact with her at the soup kitchen, but she was never as communicative with me (or anyone else, from my observations) as she had been in those initial months.

Henry

Henry was also a workfare worker. In his early twenties, he was extremely thin, had many teeth missing, and eyes that often looked dazed. Henry worked in the kitchen for six months, then left for California. He came back to Middle City three months later, looking even sicker than he did when he left. He told me that a person could starve in California. He soon after left the soup kitchen community, after coming to work high on drugs several mornings. Henry and I still talk to each other when we meet in Middle City, although he is no longer a regular soup kitchen guest.

Ralph

I first met Ralph while interviewing him for the survey in November. Ralph was in his midthirties. He told me that he had recently gotten out of prison in a neighboring state. He said that he came to Middle City to stay out of trouble. He lived alone in a rooming house, and most of his day was spent in walking around. I maintained contact with Ralph throughout the study, and he is still a regular soup kitchen guest. He was one of the group of young adults who ate together each day, coming to the soup kitchen a little before noon for about forty-five minutes of socializing before the meal.

Pedro

Pedro was a Puerto Rican man in his early fifties whom I met as a workfare worker. He later developed cancer in his back and could no longer work, but he was still a daily guest at the soup kitchen. Pedro lived alone in the Hotel Paradise. He told me that he was in Middle City for the *tranquilidad* (tranquility) that he had not found in other cities. Pedro appeared to be literate in Spanish, but his knowledge of English was limited to some friendly greetings. Aside from his hours in the soup kitchen, he spent most of his days and evenings standing outside of the Hotel Paradise, talking to the other men and intently watching the activities on Main Street. Pedro died of cancer in the summer of 1986.

Kate

At first glance, Kate appeared to be a very attractive young woman in her midtwenties. She was slim and had long dark hair and a pretty smile. A kitchen worker, she lived at the Hotel Paradise with her boyfriend. Once I got to know Kate a little better, I could see how tired-looking she was. She had several teeth missing, which contributed to her unhealthy-looking appearance. Kate told me soon after we met that she was an alcoholic. She had once been married and had a job as a clerical worker in a nearby university. Those days were gone, however, and in the years of knowing Kate I saw her go on and off the wagon. Her pattern was to drink until she needed to be hospitalized, to stay sober for a month or two, and then to resume drinking.

Esther

Esther was one of the women in her fifties who sat at the table nearest the kitchen each day. She was severely disabled with arthritis, as well as a congenital hip impairment. She came to the soup kitchen each day on the Dial-A-Ride van, which transported her from her home in Windy Heights, where she lived with her adult sons. She was a high school graduate, and she occasionally typed letters for the soup kitchen. She was a member of the class in community counseling all three times it was given. Esther was one of the most consistent soup kitchen guests; she spent three to four hours a day in the dining room, five days a week.

Alan

Alan was a man in his twenties who told me that his problems in life began as a child after he had a severe fever. He was a tall man with a red beard and a friendly smile. He was a friend of the Gamache family, and often played with the young children of the soup kitchen. He was a member of the community resources class, and became active in a community tenants' rights group. Now he occasionally has a job on the second or third shift, which he is able to hold for a few months.

Sue

I remember the first day I met Sue. At first she looked drunk, but then she explained to all around her that she had an equilibrium problem as a result of a blow to her head. She told us that she was living at the psychiatric halfway house. I noticed that she had a tracheotomy scar on her neck. During the four years I knew Sue, she moved out of the halfway house, got a boyfriend, moved into the Hotel Paradise, and had a baby. She grew stronger, and her speech became less dysarthric and more intelligible. Sue used the soup kitchen almost daily after her first time there. She was one of the most articulate and communicative of all the guests, and she was an ideal teacher of the soup kitchen culture for me.

George
George was the black man whose funeral was described at the beginning of the study. He was an example of one of the almost homeless people who spent their days getting shelter from the soup kitchen in the morning and the public library in the afternoon. George was a friendly man who appeared to have a circle of friends among the other single men and women in their forties and fifties.

Beth
Beth was one of the isolates of the soup kitchen. I noticed her as a daily guest in the spring of 1985, and our relationship developed during that fall. She lived alone, and worked in the kitchen of a restaurant for four hours a day. She sat alone in the soup kitchen, unless I took a seat near her. Beth was in her early fifties. She spoke of one adult daughter, but from her conversation it appeared that she spent many lonely hours by herself. She was a member of the community counseling class, and told me almost daily how much the classes meant to her.

Issues and Dilemmas of Participant Observation

It is probably not possible for any researcher to have rapport with all members of a community, and the people with whom he develops the most in-depth relationships (his key informants) tend to come from only some of the groups within the community. Therefore it is the responsibility of the researcher to acknowledge which groups of people have been most represented in the study. In this study, the relationships were most firmly established with the white women, Puerto Rican men, men and women of the workfare group, and members of some of the extended family groups at the soup kitchen. Those who tended not to become key informants were some of the young men and women who came to the dining room right before the meal was served, and those who much of the time appeared to be inaccessible because they were actively pacing or hallucinating, or were known to be violent toward those who approached them.

However, even those who appeared violent or disturbed some of the time were friendly and communicative to me on some days in the soup kitchen.

In a recent study on homelessness in New York City, Ellen Baxter and Kim Hopper (1981) found that most of the homeless people they got to know were friendly and eager for some companionship. Because one of the motivating factors in utilizing the soup kitchen is the need for companionship, it was relatively easy to make the initial contact with the guests. However, I found, as did Baxter and Hopper with the homeless, that a person's situation (his *story*) really came out over a long period of repeated contacts. As a matter of fact, hearing a person's story over a period of time in the soup kitchen was helpful in learning about the life cycles, such as the cycle of drinking and not drinking, or the cycle of employment and unemployment that regularly occurred to the guests. The extended time period also enabled the guests to trust me and share parts of their life histories with me once they saw that I was capable of respecting confidences.

The life-history method (Langness 1965) of gathering an extensive record of an individual has enabled anthropologists and others to explore cultures little described or understood, as James Freeman demonstrated in his book *Untouchable* (1979), a description of members of the low-caste Bauri group in a village in India. Although I was not able to compile complete life histories of any of the guests, I was able to gather biographical sketches of some people in order to understand what events and circumstances had led each person to the point at which I saw him in the soup kitchen. As in most life histories, all of the names and specific places have been changed to protect the anonymity of everyone in the soup kitchen.

An interesting issue that emerged in my work was whether or not to speak to the guests away from the soup kitchen. By the end of four years I had become an acquaintance of most of them. Yet I sensed, upon seeing some of the guests on the streets or in the stores of Middle City, that they would prefer not to recognize me. I always respected this, and if the guests tried not to look at me, I also pretended I had never seen them before.

Two further potential dilemmas involved the issues of drugs and child abuse in the soup kitchen. In their conversations, guests occasionally referred to who had illicit drugs and where they could be bought in Middle City. I never said anything to anyone about these conversations, and in addition felt I was being included in on what was probably community knowledge among many of the poor in Middle City.

I found the issue of violence toward children much more difficult to handle. As an anthropologist, my job was to understand the culture of the soup kitchen in all of its dimensions, but ethically I felt I could not stand by and watch a child being beaten. One day, a young mother in the dining room was becoming more and more upset with her two-year-old for not "obeying" her. She took the child upstairs to "teach her a lesson." The young woman paced the floor, took off her belt, and was flushed and sweaty with anger. In order to try to reduce the young woman's stress with her child, I asked her if I could help (this did temporarily dampen her anger), and later told the soup kitchen director that I thought that perhaps that young woman needed more help than she was already receiving (she was already a client of the child protective agency).

One of the challenges of doing an ethnography "at home" rather than in another culture is the illusion that we understand the meanings of people's behavior just because we speak a common language and live in the same community. In a very interesting discussion of the issues of urban anthropology in American society, Paul Bohannan (1981) describes the work of anthropologists in an "unseen community"—a group of elderly poor in single-room-occupancy hotels in center city San Diego. He describes his own first reactions and those of his research team as "There, but for the grace of God, go I." Later, especially through their debriefing team meetings, the researchers were able to guard against the tendency to overidentify with the informants, and fall into the trap of projecting the anthropologists' own feelings onto them. These cautions are relevant to the work in the soup kitchen since it was possible to identify with the young unemployed in the soup kitchen and project onto them my own sense of the frustration and boredom I would have felt in a similar situation. I later came to appreciate the variation in the feelings toward employment and unemployment that they seemed to have. Bohannan's use of the debriefing sessions would be a helpful tool in future soup kitchen research, as a brake to the tendency to project one's own feelings onto people who look and act not too differently from oneself.

Gatekeepers of the Soup Kitchen

Throughout the study it was necessary to develop and maintain rapport with both the guests and the administration. The latter group, sometimes referred to in anthropology as the gatekeepers of a field setting because they can either accept or reject the entry of the field researcher, included the directors, the ministers, and the City Ministry committee of the church. As is rather typical of institutions in the contemporary United States, these roles were occupied by a changing cadre of people during the three-year period. This meant that it was necessary to explain my presence in the soup kitchen several times, to a variety of gatekeepers, over the course of the study.

I entered the Tabernacle Soup Kitchen in the early spring of 1983, at which time Jean, the founding director, was deciding to leave her position. Jean welcomed me to the soup kitchen because she saw me, I believe, as someone with whom she could vent her many frustrations, which she felt were caused by the church administration. Jean gave me a free hand to socialize with guests and to do some preliminary quantitative research. The second director, Christine, came in the fall of 1983. While she appeared to accept my presence as a given within the soup kitchen, she was very definite in her desire to know about everything I was doing there. Eventually we developed a mutual respect. Also during the fall of 1983, a nurse began to work at the soup kitchen, and it was necessary to gain her trust and respect, since I thought it would be important to be involved in her health-related projects.

During the time in the soup kitchen, I maintained rapport with

one minister and two assistant ministers (none of whom is still at the church). My only direct conflict came when one of the assistant ministers confronted me about the lack of content regarding "spirituality" in a class on community resources I had proposed to teach to some of the guests. It was his belief that everything done within the soup kitchen should have an explicitly spiritual (by which he meant Christian) component. Since I could not provide any religious teaching within my classes, the chief minister suggested a compromise—that the assistant minister meet with the class after I had assembled the group. We both agreed to the plan, but the assistant left the church before the classes began.

The third group of gatekeepers was the City Ministry committee of Saint Mary's Church. This was composed of a group of fifteen parishioners whose job it was to oversee the soup kitchen. I met with this group three times, presenting materials, seeking their approval for my activities, and providing them with the results of the projects. They were always cordial and appeared to appreciate the follow-up presentations on the projects.

In order to work within a setting such as a soup kitchen, it is important to establish, early in one's contact, what kinds of reciprocal relationships one will have with the guests and administrators. I was able to demonstrate my ability to act as an advocate for individual guests—for example, by helping a woman find emergency shelter, helping a man living in a crowded single room look for an apartment, or helping another man make contact with an alcohol treatment center. I was able to be an individual advocate for guests at the soup kitchen almost every day I was there. However, the one issue in this that must be faced is that the problems of guests of a soup kitchen do not lend themselves to quick, one-day solutions. It was therefore important to let the director know what I was doing, so that she might be aware of any follow-up work to be done. Another issue for me was that I did not want to cast myself into a social work role (a role with which I was already well acquainted), which would, I believe, have cut me off from relationships with people who did not want "help." The individual advocacy work did prove to be an effective way to know the guests, and to reciprocate for the time they spent with me each day. I was also able to serve as an interpreter for the Spanish-speaking guests (approximately 20 percent of the guests) who wanted to communicate with the director or an agency outside of the soup kitchen. For several months the director asked me to translate the menu daily as she announced it at noontime. I was also able to reciprocate with the soup kitchen as a whole by presenting them with the written results of two studies of their guests (see Chapter 5) and by conducting classes in community resources for the guests.

Demographic, Health, and Social Surveys

Quantitative methods included a brief survey of 104 guests of the soup kitchen, and in-depth interviews with 74 guests, in order to discover the social, economic, and health issues in their lives. One is easily overwhelmed by the obvious problems of 100 or more guests, but it is important to document their conditions. Documentation was undertaken to assist the Tabernacle Soup Kitchen, and other soup kitchens that may benefit from data systematically obtained.

In the spring of 1983 a brief questionnaire was administered to 104 guests in order to gather an overview of their characteristics and of their patterns of utilization of the soup kitchen. Within three days, almost all had answered a one-page questionnaire (see Chapter 3 for the results of both surveys), demonstrating their willingness, given the proper conditions, to provide some information about themselves.

In the fall of 1983 an in-depth interview schedule was administered to 74 guests by a team of health and social service professionals. It was important that these interviews, administered in English and Spanish, be nonthreatening in tone, and not interfere with the 12:30 meal. The variables addressed by the research were: demographic characteristics of sex, ethnicity, age, and household membership; social characteristics of income, employment, housing, and education; health status including physical health, mental health, access to health care, and the use of services; and soup kitchen utilization, including time of arrival, number of days of use, and a twenty-four-hour diet-recall. These variables were measured and analyzed in order to gain a picture of the guests and their use of the soup kitchen. The demographic characteristics were designed to answer the fundamental question about who comes to the soup kitchen. Do a relatively higher proportion of those living alone come? Does the Tabernacle Soup Kitchen primarily attract people who are younger than forty? What are the implications of the demographic profile of the soup kitchen, and is this typical of soup kitchens in general or peculiar to only this one?

Soup Kitchen Research and Anthropology

The research in the soup kitchen sought to answer the questions of who the guests of the soup kitchen are and why they come to the

Tabernacle Soup Kitchen, day after day, for several hours at a time, and sit in a barren dining room? The research was undertaken with the belief that the guests in the soup kitchen knew why they came, and the ethnography was meant "to learn and formulate what others in a sense already know" (Hymes 1969: 53).

The quantitative survey research sought to provide a broad picture of the range of people and their life situations. If, for example, the research could document the preponderance of young people in the soup kitchen, what could this point to in terms of the future social, political, and economic planning for young people who are guests at soup kitchens?

In many ways, soup kitchen research can fall under the rubric of applied anthropology, which occurs "when anthropologists utilize their theoretical concepts, factual knowledge and research methods in programs meant to ameliorate contemporary social, economic and technological problems" (Foster 1969: vii).

The insights gained from this study are meant to address themselves to the amelioration of those conditions which lead people to become guests of the soup kitchen: poverty, loneliness, poor educational and employment opportunities, and ill health. The study is an attempt to know people on their own turf—away from the hospital, welfare office, or mental health clinic setting, from where so much of our "knowledge" of the poor comes.

Anthropologists can use their skill in observing, describing, and understanding groups of people in order to enable the unseen, economically and politically marginal groups in contemporary society to have a voice in social policies that shape their destinies. Along with studies of the urban nomads of skid row, the elderly poor in rooms in inner cities, and elderly Jews in a community center, the soup kitchen research will, we hope, add to our store of accurate, reliable information about a largely unknown culture.

5

Profile of the Guest Population

In spite of the eighties renaissance of soup kitchens throughout the United States, there is little documentation of who comes to a soup kitchen and why. In an effort to provide accurate, reliable information, two surveys were conducted within the Tabernacle Soup Kitchen of Saint Mary's Church in Middle City, Connecticut.

The first survey of the Tabernacle Soup Kitchen was a brief, self-administered questionnaire, designed to look at the demographic characteristics of the guests. The second was a face-to-face, in-depth interview, designed to describe their demographic, social, and health conditions, as well as their patterns of utilization of the soup kitchen.

Soup kitchens are unique in contemporary life in that they offer a service without requiring eligibility procedures, paperwork, or intrusive interviews. In this way, soup kitchens offer their services to people who may be too fearful, discouraged, disoriented, or hostile to participate in the lengthy and invasive protocol of the contemporary social agency. The two surveys therefore had to be conducted without violating the integrity and spirit of the soup kitchen. The guests were not pressured to participate in either survey, and participation was in no way presented as a prerequisite to being served the meal. Since the second in-depth interview took approximately forty-five minutes to administer, it was also important not to interfere with the guests' 12:30 meal. Therefore, almost all of the interviews were started by 11:30 A.M. or earlier. This did create a slight bias in sampling toward those guests who used the soup kitchen for one or more hours. In both surveys, there is a bias towards those guests who were willing to be interviewed.

Brief Survey of 104 Guests

In March, 1983, in order to gather basic demographic information, 104 surveys were distributed to the people who ate at the Tabernacle Soup Kitchen. The survey itself was implemented with the help of several guests who regularly ate there; they asked the rest of the people to participate. The survey was anonymous and was read to the people who could not read or write. It was written and administered in English and Spanish. Table 5.1 summarizes the findings of the survey.

During the three days of the survey, the number of guests eating at the soup kitchen was 80, 93, and 108. Although the daily total census includes children, those under 14 were not interviewed in either of the surveys discussed here, and information about the children of the soup kitchen came through their parents. There tended to be between five and ten children at the soup kitchen daily, although these numbers vary. The participation of 104 guests in the survey suggests an almost universal sample, if the guests during those days were primarily the same people. The large number of respondents also indicates that, given the right circumstances, quantitative data can emerge from the soup kitchen.

The results of the brief survey indicate a relatively young population (73 percent are under forty). The ethnic distribution of white 74 percent, Hispanic (primarily Puerto Rican) 24 percent, and black 2 percent, indicates a higher proportion of Hispanics than the 8 percent reported by the U.S. Census for 1980 in Middle City. Within the area of education, 39 percent of the guests were at least high school graduates, and, of those, 13 percent had some college.

Table 5.1
Results of Brief Survey of 104 Guests

Age	Number	%	Ethnicity	Number	%
<16	3	3	White	77	74
17–25	39	38	Hispanic	25	24
26–40	33	32	Black	2	2
41–55	18	17			
>55	5	5			

Level of Education			Cooking Facilities?		
< 8 grade	12	12	Yes	82	79
8 grade	19	18	No	22	21
9–11 grade	23	22			
H.S. grad	27	26			
Some college	9	9			
College grad	4	4			

Time of Arrival at S.K.*		cum %	Times per Week at S.K.*		cum %
9:00	4	4	< One time	8	8
9:30	2	6	One time	9	9
10:00	11	17	Two times	13	13
10:30	1	18	Three times	11	11
11:00	22	39	Four times	8	8
11:30	1	51	Five times	16	15
12:00	14	64	Six times*	26	25
12:30	7	71	Missing	13	13
Missing	31	100			

Mean # hours:1 hour, 45 minutes; mean times per week: 3.69
*4 hours is the maximum number. *6 is maximum days.

Reasons for Coming
(may have more than one answer)

For company	59	57	Workfare	15	14
Unemployed	59	57	Disability	15	14
Hungry	54	52	No cooking facilities	12	12
Save money	35	34			
Children to feed	25	24			

It would be interesting to explore circumstances that led this latter group of people to become guests of the soup kitchen.

Of the 104 guests, 22 (21 percent) said that they had no cooking facilities, so the soup kitchen was an important source for a hot meal for those guests who lived in rooms without a stove. The question regarding cooking facilities was somewhat ambiguous, since it became clear through the second survey and through the ethnographic data that for some guests having a hot plate in their room constituted "cooking facilities." Therefore, 21 percent may be an undercount of the number of guests who were without access to a stove and refrigerator.

The Tabernacle Soup Kitchen is open six days a week, Monday through Saturday, from 9 A.M. to 1 P.M. The mean number of days of soup kitchen attendance for the guests was 3.39 days, and 50 percent of the guests arrived by 11:30 A.M. This appears to reflect a rather intensive utilization of the soup kitchen.

The guests were asked why they came to the soup kitchen by an open-ended question and by checking off responses from a list that was derived from the pretest of the survey. The dominant reasons reported were for the company, because they were unemployed, and because they were hungry. The high percentage of guests who said that they came to the soup kitchen for socializing confirms the impressions drawn from the ethnographic data that the soup kitchen is important in the social life of the guest, as well as being an important nutritional resource.

In-Depth Survey of 74 Guests

In October, November, and December, 1983, information was collected about 74 guests of the Tabernacle Soup Kitchen. A committee consisting of the soup kitchen nurse, a physician, the soup kitchen director, and myself (an anthropologist) constructed a 45-minute interview schedule which was designed to evaluate the health and social condition of the guest. A small grant from a private foundation provided funds in order to give each guest who agreed to be interviewed a health-promotion gift of an oral thermometer, accompanied by an illustrated, bilingual (Spanish and English) page of instructions. The questions were written in English and Spanish, and the interviews were carried out by public health nurses, social workers, and several medical anthropologists. Within three months, 74 Tabernacle Soup Kitchen guests had discussed their health and social situation through the community survey.

Most of the interviews took place at the soup kitchen, in one of the rooms of Saint Mary's Church, adjacent to the dining room. These rooms afforded privacy for the interview while offering the guest the comfort of a familiar setting. Ten interviews were conducted at the Center for English as a Second Language in Middle City, for those soup kitchen guests who were studying English and who arrived at the soup kitchen daily at 12:30, just in time for the meal. In this way, we were able to include some guests who were regular users of the soup kitchen but did not spend more than one hour there.

In October, November, and December, 1983, an average of 80, 85, and 87 guests were fed daily, including children. It appears, therefore, that the 74 survey respondents represented a fairly high proportion of the entire universe of possible respondents. It is felt that the community survey respondent was representative of the Tabernacle Soup Kitchen, with a slightly higher proportion of frequent and longer-staying guests, Hispanics, and workfare workers. It was decided to include the latter group, since workfare workers are usually guests before and after their workfare assignment at the soup kitchen, and are guests on their days off.

Demographic Characteristics

Table 5.2 summarizes some of the primary demographic characteristics of the soup kitchen guests who participated in the survey.

The distribution of males and females in the soup kitchen indicates that two-fifths of the population was male and three-fifths was female. The greater number of females may have been due to the group of young mothers who came to the soup kitchen daily with their children. The sex distribution of the Tabernacle Soup Kitchen

Table 5.2
Demographic Characteristics of Surveyed Guests

	Number	%*
Sex		
Male	30	41
Female	44	59
Ethnicity		
White	50	68
Hispanic	23	31
Black	1	1
Age		
14–19	8	11
20–29	26	35
30–39	14	19
40–49	11	15
50–59	8	11
60–76	7	10
Mean age: 35; median age: 31		
Living Arrangements		
Alone	28	39
With children, grandchildren	19	26
With spouse	8	11
With friends	10	14
With parents	6	8
With siblings	2	3
In halfway house	1	1

*Percent may be > 100 due to rounding.

was more evenly divided between male and female than in some inner-city soup kitchens, which tend to be more predominantly male, based on observations in more urban areas in Connecticut.

The majority (65 percent) of surveyed guests of the Tabernacle Soup Kitchen were under forty years old. This finding contrasts with the earlier images of soup kitchens as primarily serving elderly populations. This large group of young people is of interest in that it also reflects, for the most part, a population that is not employed. The health and ethnographic data reveal that many of these young people have serious physical and mental health problems which currently impede their employability. Many have become discouraged in their ability to ever secure and hold down a job.

There are many similarities between the population of the soup kitchen and groups that are disproportionately poor in Middle City, including female-headed households, people living alone, and members of the Hispanic population. The relatively high degree of participation of Hispanics in the soup kitchen contrasts with their underutilization of many other health and social services in the area (Boujouen and Newton 1984). Perhaps the nature of the soup kitchen service, which does not require English language ability, conveys a compatible ambiance for the Hispanic population. The Hispanic respondents (31 percent) in the survey may also represent a slight oversampling, since some of the interviewing was done in the English as a Second Language class.

It should be noted that the twenty-six respondents who reported having children and grandchildren with them did not include the soup kitchen guests who had children under eighteen who were now living apart from them. The question about the number of children proved to be, in fact, one of the most difficult questions to ask on the survey, since some of the women had had children taken from them by the state.

The soup kitchen population included 10 percent of people over sixty years of age. There was one other year-round community feeding program: one directed toward the elderly. It would perhaps be of further interest to explore how the elderly population who do eat at the soup kitchen choose this rather than one of the nutrition sites for the elderly.

Income

The majority of the surveyed soup kitchen guests received some sort of assistance through general assistance, state welfare (usually Aid to Families with Dependent Children, AFDC), supplemental security income (SSI), and social security. Many of the respondents receiving general assistance (commonly referred to as town welfare), were a part of the workfare program, which places people in public service positions for fifteen to twenty hours weekly so they can "pay off" their welfare grant. There were also four respondents who were working in the competitive job market, either in jobs that were on the second or third shift, or jobs that required good weather.

The amount of money the guests received from any of these programs fell well below the poverty line. For example, in 1984 the federal poverty line for an individual was $4,980 annually. This contrasts with the $3,588 received annually by a town welfare recipient, and the $3,900 received by a SSI recipient. The poverty line for a two-person household was $6,720, in contrast to the $4,416 annually for the AFDC household of the same size. Finally, Social Security payments vary with the amount of time the individual has worked, with a minimum payment of $325 a month ($3,900 annually).

In addition to the meager income of most of the guests, there were further financial issues that complicated their lives. For example, a recipient of town welfare received $95 monthly, and the town paid a maximum of $200 a month in rent directly to the landlord. In Middle City, the only housing available for $200 a month were rooms in a single-room-occupancy hotel or in rooming houses with very limited cooking facilities. A family on AFDC, consisting of a mother and child, received $368 monthly. One of the issues here was that the state requires separate bedrooms for parent and child, and two-bedroom apartments are not available in Middle City for less than $300 a month (Broomfield 1985). Therefore, often more of a person's financial assistance is used for housing and less is available for food (even with food stamps) than state and federal guidelines would indicate on paper.

Table 5.3 indicates the source of income of the surveyed guests.

Housing

An individual's income is closely tied to the kind of housing available, and Middle City has a limited number of low-cost rentals. Most of the guests (68 percent) lived in apartments in either the downtown area near the soup kitchen or in one of the three housing

Table 5.3
Source of Income

Program	Number	%
Town welfare	31	44
State welfare	15	21
Social Security	9	13
SSI	7	10
Unemployment Compensation	1	1
Supported by parents	2	3
Supported by spouse	2	3
Employment	4	6

projects in Middle City. The next largest group (33 percent) lived in the single-room-occupancy hotel or in a room in a rooming house.

When asked about their housing, the guests reported the following areas out of a list of fourteen possible housing problems (Table 5.4). It must be kept in mind that the list represents *perceived* problems. People who are accustomed to living with no transportation, no laundry facilities, no telephone, no refrigerator, and possibly only the use of a hot plate for cooking facilities often do not report these as problems.

The relatively high number of respondents who cited unpleasant living conditions, including the presence of cockroaches (62 percent), fear of robberies (44 percent), and too much noise (33 percent), sheds light on some of the reasons people might be eager to leave their rooms and apartments and go to the soup kitchen. Furthermore, the lack of a working refrigerator, reported by 33 percent of the respondents, and the lack of cooking facilities, reported by 24 percent, affected their ability to store food and to cook, and also contributed to their need for the soup kitchen. If a person cannot cook, he must spend a great deal more of his income on restaurant or take-out meals. In addition, food stamps cannot be used for restaurant meals, further restricting the person's food resources.

Health
We were interested in documenting the physical and mental health of the guests of the soup kitchen, as well as their access to

Table 5.4
Housing Problems Reported

Problem	Number	%
Cockroaches	45	62
No telephone*	34	47
Fear of robbery	32	44
No laundry facilities	30	41
Too much noise	30	41
No refrigerator	17	23
Inadequate heating	14	19
Inadequate toilets	13	18
Poor stairs	13	18
No one to call in emergencies	13	18
Inadequate lighting	13	18
Flies	10	14
Rats	1	1

Average number of problems: 4
*Most of the guests do not in fact have a phone.
Cooking facilities?

Yes	56	76
No	18	24

health care. Our ethnographic data indicated a great many physical and mental health problems and numerous difficulties in obtaining care. The community survey asked the guests to report on their health and their utilization of the health-care system. There are some methodological issues concerning the validity of self-reported health data as opposed to clinical. While surveys in the form of interviews are a good way to gauge a population's health in a relatively inexpensive, unobtrusive way, there have been some studies cited by Thomas Tissue (1972) which suggest disparities between health data reported in an interview and health data obtained from medical records. A more accurate term for the health assessments obtained from interviews is perhaps *perceived* health (Suchman, Phillips, and Streib 1958).

The guests were asked their height and weight, and were also asked about the presence of thirty-eight symptoms and conditions,

Table 5.5
Health Issues Reported by Surveyed Soup Kitchen Guests

Problem	Number	%
Depression	42	58
Headaches	40	55
Dental, gum	39	54
Nervousness	36	49
Backaches	29	49
Shortness of breath	27	40
Have had fracture	21	37
Vision problem	21	29
Chest pain	19	29
Suicidal thoughts, attempts	19	26
Use street drugs	12	16
Drink too much	11	15
Overweight	24	32
Underweight	3	4

including depression, nervousness, their use of street drugs, their assessment as to whether they "drink too much," and their suicidal thoughts and/or attempts. It was thought that the reporting on the use of street drugs, the excessive use of alcohol (by their own standards), and the presence of suicidal thoughts and attempts perhaps represented an underestimate of the true incidence of these occurrences. An estimate was made of the number of overweight and underweight guests, based on calculations derived from the standard that 20 percent over the ideal weight and 20 percent under the ideal weight constitutes over- and underweight respectively (Bierman 1982).

Table 5.5 summarizes the health issues of the guests of the soup kitchen.

The most prevalent symptoms and conditions in this study were the cluster of mental health problems of depression, nervousness, suicidal thoughts and attempts, use of street drugs, and excessive drinking. Of the seventy-four respondents, sixty reported having at least one of these symptoms, with a mean of 1.6 psychologically

oriented symptoms per person. The prevalence of psychological symptoms for this study is 82 percent. In their review of studies of the rates of psychological disorders, which are usually defined as neuroses, psychoses, character disorder, alcoholism, and drug abuse, Dohrenwend and Dohrenwend (1969) cite a broad range of reported psychological disorder rates in forty studies, from 1 percent to 60 percent. A more recent review (Eisenberg 1977) indicates the prevalence of psychiatric disorders in the general population to be 15 to 20 percent. Most of the studies demonstrated a positive relationship between low socioeconomic status and rates of mental disorder. In a study of psychological problems of patients in a general medical practice in Middle City, Glasser (1976) reports a rate of 8 percent of the 4,801 patients seen over a four-year period who mentioned mental health problems in the course of a general medical interview. The rate of 81 percent of guests reporting symptoms of mental health problems, therefore, is considerably higher than published reports

Table 5.6
Guests with Mental Health Problems*

Group	Number	% of Group
Sex		
Male	24	83
Female	36	82
Ethnicity		
White	42	86
Hispanic	17	74
Black	1	100
Age		
14–19	5	83
20–29	25	96
30–39	12	92
40–49	7	64
50–59	5	63
60 +	4	67
Living Arrangements		
Alone	22	82
With children, grandchildren	15	79
With spouse	8	100
With friends	8	80
With siblings	4	67
In halfway house	1	100

*In this study, a guest with mental health problems is counted as any guest who answered in the affirmative to the existence of one or more of the following conditions: depression, nervousness, suicidal thoughts or attempts, use of street drugs, and excessive drinking.

in the United States population in general, and in Middle City in particular. These symptoms may be seen as both concomitants of poverty itself and as some of the factors contributing to a person's inability to work and subsequent reliance on public assistance.

Table 5.6 illustrates the relationship of the symptoms of mental health problems and the various demographic characteristics of the guests.

Although none of the relationships are statistically significant due to the small sample size, the highest percentage of mental health problems appeared to occur among guests under forty years of age. This finding is corroborated by the ethnographic data of this study, which suggests the utilization of the soup kitchen by young people with a variety of serious social and emotional problems. The study findings also support the growing concern expressed in psychiatric literature about the increasing number of young people who may be chronically and seriously psychiatrically disabled (Segal and Baumohl 1982).

Dental and gum disease are considered the most prevalent of all chronic health problems in the United States (Health System Plan for Eastern Connecticut 1979–1983), and dental and gum diseases are definitely related to a person's income (Lerner 1975). The rate of 54 percent of dental and gum problems reported on by guests of the soup kitchen conforms to other reports of dental health of people in poverty. It should also be noted that some of the guests who had had all of their teeth extracted (some at a relatively young age) and had no dentures usually did not report any dental problems.

Poverty and obesity for adult females has long been reported to be positively correlated in the United States (Weil 1984), due in part to the quality of the food and lack of activity among low-income groups (McElroy and Townsend 1979). The 32 percent rate of obesity based on reported height and weight of the guests falls in the upper range of the 10 percent to 40 percent rates of obesity reported in various studies of the general population (Kohrs 1979).

The remaining health problems reported by the guests are difficult to compare to the rest of the population, since they refer to past conditions (accidents and fractures) and common symptoms, including headaches and backaches.

When asked if they had a doctor or dentist, 53 percent of the guests reported that they had a doctor, and 28 percent reported that they had a dentist. The lack of a regular dentist reported by 72 percent of the respondents indicates a significant lack of dental care, consistent with the relatively high percentage reporting dental and gum problems. When asked if they had trouble obtaining health care, 24 (35 percent) of those answering the question cited problems of finances, difficulty in obtaining an appointment, English language, and transportation problems. Some of the guests appeared to feel that they had "no problem" in obtaining medical care, even though we knew from our interactions with them that their sole source of medical care was through the hospital emergency room, with little or no follow-up care. If they were recipients of town welfare, they had to obtain prior permission, which is granted on an emergency basis only, for each medical and dental visit. At the time of the study, there was no clinic care for dental or medical problems, except for a well-baby and prenatal clinic. Since the time of the study, a free health clinic has become available for several days per week for low-income people.

The guests were also asked about their past or current involvement with social agencies. In the area of mental health, twenty-one (28 percent) said that they were clients of the local mental health clinic. This contrasts with the 81 percent who reported one or more symptoms of mental health problems.

Education and Employment

The majority (68 percent) of the guests had not graduated from high school, and most were not involved with a school program at the time of the study, with the exception of the English as a Second Language students. In the area of employment, 4 percent of the guests reported having a job. However, some were employed in jobs that are usually not counted within conventional descriptions of employment. These guests were most often engaged in local, state, or federally supported work programs or were women who perceived themselves as homemakers.

The ethnographic data indicate that jobs and job training were important topics of conversation among the guests. Although the recent employment history of the guests might be bleak, for most of them the dreams of a job were not gone. When asked what kind of job training they might be interested in, the vast majority (92 percent) cited some kind of further education or job training in areas including computers, nursing, the arts, or the armed services. The guests were asked their own perceptions of their difficulties in obtaining employment. Problems cited included health, advanced age, lack of qualifications, lack of jobs, unavailability of transportation, inadequate English proficiency, and children in need of child care. It appears, from knowing the guests, that their perceived job problems are indeed true impediments in today's job market. Furthermore, many of the guests appeared to have lost the confidence they may have once had in their ability to be successful in employment. The ethnographic data indicate that the few guests who do reenter the job market do so with a lot of support from family, friends, and soup kitchen staff. Recently, a project within the Tabernacle Soup Kitchen to train kitchen workers in the workfare program demonstrated that with supportive structured training, designed with the needs of the guests in mind, long-term unemployed people could reenter the competitive job market successfully.

Soup Kitchen Utilization

As a part of the atmosphere of nonharassment, guests are not asked to sign in in most soup kitchens. It is usually difficult, therefore, to assess the extent of soup kitchen utilization. This study did ask each guest at what hour they usually arrived and how many times a week they usually came to the soup kitchen. The mean number of hours spent in the soup kitchen was two (out of a maximum of four) and the mean number of days of attendance was four (out of a possible six). The data indicate a rather intensive use of the soup kitchen.

Who were the guests who tended to spend the most time in the soup kitchen? It was hypothesized that the most regular user was the person most in need of its nutritional and social aspects. The regular user is defined, for purposes of analysis, as the guest who spent at least two hours in the soup kitchen, four days a week. It was thought that the regular user would be most likely to have no cooking facilities and have a greater number of symptoms of mental health problems.

The only statistically significant relationship found was that Hispanics were not regulars (only 19 percent of the Hispanic guests

were regulars). This was probably related to the fact that the Hispanic guests came to the soup kitchen close to the mealtime.

In addition to the utilization in terms of hours and days, it would
be of interest to know something of the *cycle* of use. In other words,
for how long does a guest come to the soup kitchen? This information, like utilization, is generally difficult to obtain, since soup kitchens do not require their guests to sign in.

The study, however, was able to estimate the cycle of use for the
guests of the Tabernacle Soup Kitchen. In December, 1983, we
knew the names of 68 of the 74 respondents of the community
survey. One year later we knew that 26 (38 percent) of the 68 guests
were still utilizing the soup kitchen with some degree of regularity.
Two years later we knew that 24 (35 percent) of the guests on the
original list were still guests. Two who had appeared on the original
list were not guests one year later, but were guests two years later.
Of those people who were no longer soup kitchen guests, we knew
that some had left the area or had moved to an apartment no longer
convenient to the soup kitchen, some had found employment, and
some had stopped coming although they still lived in the area. We
also knew of four guests who were utilizing other soup kitchens
elsewhere in the state after leaving the Tabernacle Soup Kitchen.

Approximately one-third of the guests form a more or less permanent group of people in the dining room. This has implications
for the planning of programs based on long-term relationships with
the guests. It also means that the majority of guests stay in the soup
kitchen for less than a year. Although there is no actual quantified
data, my observations indicated that most guests maintain a regular
soup kitchen schedule for three to six months when the soup kitchen
serves important nutritional and social needs in their lives. I suspect
that soup kitchens in larger metropolitan areas, where the guests
come from a more transient population, have a more rapid turnover.

Nutrition

How did soup kitchen use affect the nutrition of the guests? This
is an important but complex question. The major difficulty was in
gathering reliable data from the guests as to what they had eaten in

the previous 24 hours. Most appeared to have only a vague recollection of the events of the previous day, which is not surprising given the difficult life circumstances of most of the guests. For those who had eaten a soup kitchen meal on the previous day, it was possible to check the menu of the soup kitchen for that day, and thereby gain more accurate knowledge of the guests' food intake.

Each respondent was asked to recall the foods he had eaten during the previous 24-hour period. Since we were not able to consistently assess the quantities of foods eaten, we were only able to establish the variety eaten by the guests. We calculated the number of food groups not eaten during the 24-hour diet-recall for each guest by utilizing the guidelines of the American Diabetes Association and the American Dietetic Association booklet *The Exchange List for Meal Planning*. A guest was said to have a missing food group in his diet-recall if he had eaten no foods at all from that group. The missing food groups were calculated with the consultation of Sarah Winter, a community nutritionist. Of the 72 diet-recalls, 31 were for days that included the soup kitchen meal for the respondent, and 41 were for days that did not include the soup kitchen meal. This means that there was some basis on which to compare the nutritional significance of the soup kitchen meal. A diet-recall would not have included the meal if the previous 24 hours included a Sunday, when the soup kitchen was closed, or a day the person had not come to the soup kitchen.

Table 5.7 indicates the food groups that were most often missing from the diets of the guests. Of those guests (31) for whom the diet-recall included a soup kitchen meal, 61 percent had one or fewer food groups missing from their diet-recall, whereas only 24 percent of those guests (41) for whom the diet-recall did not include the soup kitchen meal had one or fewer missing food groups. This relationship was statistically significant ($p < .002$). In other words, the addition of the soup kitchen meal to the guest's diet tended to increase the variety of foods eaten.

The nutrition data, although limited to food variety, reveal that the soup kitchen meal presents a real benefit for the guest, although this is an area which could be explored in greater depth. The data

Table 5.7
Missing Food Groups in Diet Recalls

Missing Group	Number	% of Recalls
Fruit	48	67
Milk	38	53
Vegetable	32	44
Meat	9	13
Bread	2	3

Mean number of missing food groups: 1.7

do point to the importance of the inclusion of fruit, milk, and vegetables in the preparation of the soup kitchen meal. I suggest that any further work on assessing the nutrition of the guests repeat several diet-recalls with a smaller sample of guests, so that the recall itself becomes more reliable and begins to include quantities of food.

Summary

Despite the growing phenomenon of soup kitchens, little has been known about who goes to them and why. The two surveys reported on here demonstrate that it is possible to collect basic demographic and health information from the guests, without violating the integrity of the soup kitchen.

The results of both the brief spring survey and the in-depth fall survey of the Tabernacle Soup Kitchen document the existence of economic, health, housing, education, and employment problems facing the guests. Almost every guest was the recipient of an assistance program which meant that his income fell *below* the federal poverty threshold. This left the guest with little money for food and shelter. Soup kitchen attendance can therefore be seen as a temporary solution to the guest's daily needs of food and shelter in a safe, friendly environment.

Of particular interest is the high rate of symptoms of mental health problems that emerged from the health data. These health findings can be viewed, at least in part, as both a result and a cause of the economic and employment problems facing the guests. The areas of mental health and employment need to be further addressed by the community health and human services.

The soup kitchen has come to have an important place in the daily life of a segment of the poor in Middle City. The high rate of soup kitchen utilization of this group of people in poverty in many ways contrasts with their lack of participation in many other health and human services. It is important to consider *why* the soup kitchen has, with few staff members and limited financial resources, experienced such success in reaching people in poverty. This success appears to be replicated in other towns throughout the state, and possibly the nation. Perhaps the attraction the soup kitchen holds for the poor offers clues for a more effective service-delivery system. The statistical data presented here provide a backdrop against which to consider the qualitative aspects of the soup kitchen, and the meaning it has for its guests.

6

Loneliness

Loneliness in life appears to be a driving force in bringing people to the soup kitchen. Loneliness may be conceptualized as a feeling of apartness due to a lack in the quantity or quality of social relationships, which results in an unpleasant feeling and a need for others (Peplau and Perlman 1982). The lives of the guests have often been plagued with losses: of family members; of friends who have had violent, premature deaths; of children who have been removed by the state; of spouses who have left; and of jobs lost or never had. The soup kitchen offers people an opportunity to be surrounded by others and the potential of having some human interaction. The kind of interaction that often tends to take place in the dining room may be thought of as *sociability*, which is interaction for its own sake, without the emotional impact of long-term relationships (Keenan 1982).

The atmosphere of sociability in the dining room occurs because people perceive the soup kitchen as a safe, nondemanding environment and enter the dining room each day in sufficient numbers and for several hours at a time. The safety of the environment is enhanced by the predictability of the routine: coffee and doughnuts are available from 9 A.M. until noon, and there is a hot meal at 12:30 P.M. The guests usually gravitate to "their" table, whether it is toward a loosely knit group of friends or acquaintances, or to a table all by themselves. With the exception of people who enter with specific groups of friends, guests of the Tabernacle Soup Kitchen tend not to know each other's names.

The soup kitchen offers us an almost infinite number of examples of people in search of ways to alleviate their sense of loneliness. Almost every guest I came to know expressed the desire to meet people as a reason for being in the dining room. In the brief survey reported on in Chapter 5, the majority of the guests cited "for the company" as a reason for coming to the soup kitchen.

The following vignettes of guests illustrate some of the most dramatic uses of the soup kitchen as a way of coping with loneliness. The vignettes are grouped by those in which the loneliness of the guest appeared caused by or exacerbated by a major crisis or dislocation before he or she arrived at the soup kitchen, and those in which the guest's life appeared to be characterized by chronic loneliness.

Lives in Crisis and Dislocation

Sue: Recovering from a Coma

Sue was an almost daily soup kitchen regular, who first came in the winter of 1983. She was twenty-four years old, and as described in Chapter 4, had difficulty walking and had a large tracheotomy scar on her neck. She spoke in a dysarthric manner even when sober, and wore clothes that were several sizes too small for her. Sue began coming when she was a resident of the local halfway house for former psychiatric patients. She was to do twenty hours of volunteer work as a child care worker at the soup kitchen, according to rules of the halfway house. Sue was soon asked to leave the house, but remained a soup kitchen regular afterward.

Sue had a soup kitchen routine. Each morning she arrived at about ten o'clock, and sat at the table nearest the coffee and doughnuts. This table was usually occupied by older alcoholic men, young white men and women, and black and Puerto Rican men. She would immediately begin to drink coffee, to eat the day-old doughnuts (donated by a local bakery), and smoke one cigarette after another. She often played solitaire or chatted with the other people at the table.

From our conversations over the next four years, I learned that Sue was brought up in a neighboring town, more affluent than Middle City. She left high school in the ninth grade and traveled all over the country with a drug dealer. At one point she worked in Montana clearing brush for seven dollars an hour. This was her favorite job. She also worked with retarded people in a residential facility.

About three years before, Sue had been hit on the head with a lead pipe; this resulted in her being in a coma for three months and in the hospital for two years. She attributed her memory loss and difficulty in speaking and equilibrium to the accident. Sue referred to herself as "brain damaged." She often lamented about her life— "Why am I still alive? Why is life worth living?"

Sue had a child of about four years old who lived with her former husband. Sue's parents were dead. She had a sister in the area, who refused to visit Sue in the Hotel Paradise. The hotel is an old one, which I am told was as grand as its name in the early 1900s. Now, however, it is the home of people on general assistance, many of whom are alcoholic and/or heroin addicts. The name of the hotel is a constant source of embarrassment, especially to its female residents, since it implies a house of prostitution. When the sister did visit, Sue told me that they met in the sister's car.

Sue talked often about how depressed she was. This seemed to be her conversational overture to whoever would listen. She began her conversations with me and others with "I know that nobody likes me—everyone hates me." This appeared to be an invitation to whoever was around to assure Sue that she was liked and well thought of.

One day in June, 1983, I met Sue on the street several hours after the soup kitchen had closed. She told me that she would never go back there because a man had insulted her. When I asked what had happened, she said that the man, who was tall, quiet, and had long blond hair, and was regarded by others as a loner, had gone into the kitchen to get more milk for the coffee. Instead of leaving the milk out, or offering Sue some, he had taken it back to the kitchen. When I asked her what his name was, she did not know. I thought at first that perhaps Sue was using this affront as a reason to leave the soup kitchen community, but then I saw her there again on a regular basis. Rather, the affront symbolized a certain kind of communication between the soup kitchen guests that can happen without words being exchanged. It points to the importance of even the most fleeting social interaction for the guest.

Sue was a guest whose social network was limited in terms of family and workplace. Although the soup kitchen offered her a place to go for several hours a day, this was not enough. She told me that the soup kitchen depressed her, and that she was bored with life. When I asked her about a job, she said that she was too disabled to work, and that she was not allowed to work on SSI (Supplemental Security Income). This was not the case, and when other guests who knew the details of the programs challenged Sue, her rationale crumbled. At times, she told me that her joys in life were drinking and getting high—although she said that the next day she was sorry.

One year after becoming a soup kitchen guest, Sue became involved with another hotel resident, Sonny, a black man in his fifties. She became pregnant, and appeared to be overjoyed by it. She told me about her pregnancy, showed me her clinic appointment cards at least three times during the same hour and was busy collecting baby clothes. She also talked about looking for an apartment outside of the hotel, saying (correctly, I believe) that if she stayed in the Hotel Paradise the state would be more likely to take the baby from her. Sue continued to go to the soup kitchen daily, in between her clinic appointments and her newly found activity regarding her pregnancy.

Mother and Daughter Waiting for Death

From the first days of the Tabernacle Soup Kitchen's existence, until six-year-old Patsy's death in November, 1983, Pat and her daughter Patsy spent their mornings at the soup kitchen. Patsy was born with cystic fibrosis, and except during her periods of hospitalization, the soup kitchen was her nursery school. Pat was a thin, nervous-looking woman in her forties, who smoked and drank coffee as she sat next to Patsy, who would be quietly coloring or playing with a toy. Although Pat was on speaking terms with most of the women of the soup kitchen, she and Patsy sat apart from the others. It appeared that Pat sought out the soup kitchen as a way of being around people, but not necessarily being involved with others in an intimate way. It seemed significant to me that several days after Patsy's death, Pat returned to the soup kitchen "just to visit." She was all dressed up, sat at a table with the older women, and spoke of how strange she felt now that she didn't have Patsy to care for day and night. After she had talked for about half an hour, she left before lunch was served. The soup kitchen had been a major focus of activity with her daughter, but now that the child was dead, the soup kitchen was no longer to be a part of her life.

Ralph: Returning from Prison

Ralph, as noted in Chapter 4, was one of the young men who used the soup kitchen on a regular basis. His toothless smile, his long, drawn face, and his bent-over walk made him look more like a man of fifty than the thirty years old he really was. Ralph arrived each day at about 11:30 and sat at a table with other young, unemployed adults. He lived at the "thieves' den."

Ralph told me that he had spent many years in prison in a neighboring state, and that he was in Middle City to try to start a new life for himself. His dream, he said, was to walk across the United States. We once had an animated conversation about an article we had both read in *National Geographic* about a couple who did that. Ralph wrote to *National Geographic*, and they responded that they would sponsor him with equipment and clothes if he undertook his walk. Two years later, he was still walking the streets of Middle City and coming to the soup kitchen each day.

Ralph told me that his work experience had been mainly in prison. He had also worked in a greenhouse and in a convalescent home. He said that he enjoyed the aide work in the home, but that he was not too interested in working for minimum wage. I wondered to myself how much success Ralph would have in finding a job. He appeared to be sick, both physically and mentally. I had seen him walking along the streets in a short-sleeved tee shirt in the middle of the winter. He always wore a cap, which seemed to add to the general impression of a person who was down and out.

Ralph was one of the few people who commented on the soup kitchen meals and on the management of the kitchen. He told me one day that he wished the meals were more "regular"—by which he said he meant meat and vegetables in separate places on the plate, rather than the casseroles which are the standard soup kitchen fare. I wondered if Ralph wasn't expressing his desire to be a part of a household where someone cooked, rather than depending on canned foods warmed over a hot plate in his room, the local dough-nut shop, or the soup kitchen. He also suggested that there be a special program for the children who often seemed to be running recklessly through the crowds of people and near the hot coffeepot.

Marilyn—Alone in Middle City

I first noticed Marilyn in May of 1983, sitting at one of the back tables with two young men in their twenties. They all seemed to be intently involved in Bible study. Marilyn was a slender woman of about forty, with long graying hair which she wore pulled back from her face. She was a nervous, yet graceful, woman who might have been very pretty if her life had been less harsh. My relationship with Marilyn began slowly. During our first conversations she appeared scared, and I did not want to cross the invisible line that allows the guests their personal space in an impersonal setting. Over the next few days, Marilyn began seeking me out. I noticed that she often had big law books and welfare policy manuals with her. She was searching for the law or policy that would say that she was eligible for a welfare program. Marilyn would often begin our contacts over the next six months by asking me to read some paragraph of "legalese" and interpret it for her.

Slowly, Marilyn's story of how she came to the soup kitchen began to emerge. She was reared in a rural community thirty miles east of Middle City, and had been married; she had two children, a boy and a girl. When the children were of school age, Marilyn was divorced from her husband and began living on Aid to Families with Dependent Children. She found, however, that she could no longer keep up her home mortgage payments, and decided to sell her house. Because the state has a lien on all property owned by welfare recipients, the state took most of the money from the sale of her house. Marilyn spoke bitterly of this, since it had forced her into a series of apartments. She told me that various landlords had accused her of not being able to control her children, and eventually she had been forced to place the children in foster care.

After her children were in foster care, Marilyn drove from state to state throughout the eastern portion of the United States in search of a state she would like. She got as far as Tennessee and then returned to the East Coast. Throughout our contact, Marilyn mentioned Georgia as a place she might like to live, and showed me a response she had received from a housing authority in Georgia, listing cities with public housing.

Sometime before or after the trip, Marilyn was hospitalized in a state psychiatric facility, for depression. She mentioned to me often how she resented people who told her that she should speak to a counselor, and that she refused to "tell a counselor the things they want to hear."

During the winter of 1983–1984, Marilyn found herself in Middle City, existing on general assistance. The only housing available to her was the hotel, or a room within an apartment (several guests told me that Middle City would designate certain apartments as "boarding homes" and pay $200 a month for rent of a single room within an ordinary apartment). Marilyn had chosen the apartment, but she complained bitterly throughout our contact that she had to share the bath and kitchen with men. From Middle City she was able to visit her children. Her daughter was in foster care in the area from which Marilyn had moved. Her son was in a psychiatric hospital for children, and was probably going to be placed in a residential program.

Throughout our contact, Marilyn lamented her situation in eloquent terms. After each conversation I wrote as much as I could remember, trying to retain the quality of the feelings she conveyed during our conversations, which almost all took place in the soup kitchen and were out of earshot of other people. One morning in early June, Marilyn said to me:

Irene, what do you think a liberated woman is? Are you a liberated woman? That's the question I'm trying to answer today. The government doesn't allow a woman to be liberated. Here I have all of these housing problems. This morning one of the men in my boardinghouse stole my yogurt I was going to have for breakfast. I have such an appetite these days. I try not to eat but I can't help it. Before, I never cared about eating. But now that I have no money—I have an appetite. The men I live with are disgusting. I have to clean up the bathroom just to go in there.

In response to something I said about work, Marilyn replied:

I used to work before I was married. I got a job in an ice cream parlor—though I had a hell of a time making change. Then I worked for a tax collector—there was a young girl in there stuffing envelopes—she used to make me so nervous. I had my kids then and I had to take my wash over to my sister's house before I went to work. Her washer didn't work well and the clothes were wet and heavy. . . . I've been cheated. I owned two houses—now I have nothing. Do you know what I really want to do? I want to learn how to be a bartender. I think I could do it. I've tried Dunkin Donuts—they won't have me. I want to move to an apartment and then get my kids back. Or maybe I'll send my résumé to Georgia. I hear it's a big state with not too many people. [They] are not taking any more applications for City Welfare, but I know they can't do that. . . . Maybe I can get married again. Irene, do you think I am marriageable material?

Each day that I saw Marilyn, she told me that her plans for going to Western City hadn't materialized. She had woken up too late to take the 8 A.M. bus, or it was raining. By mid-June, Marilyn was getting more desperate:

> Well, I hope that the Lord is listening to me—are you out there, Lord? You know, they keep on wanting me to go to counselors, but what good are counselors—can they help me get my children back or my house back? The counselors said I was depressed; of course I was depressed. They sent me to Greenville (public psychiatric hospital). Now you know it—I was in Greenville, yes, but they said that I didn't belong there and they sent me home. Do you think that my family ever helped me? No. All the time I was growing up—I was the oldest and no one ever helped me. I've been deprived of an education. Don't you think that I'm a minority? I deserve the special housing. . . .

I saw Marilyn several times on the street during the summer, still carrying her law books, and one time saying that perhaps she would sign up for the licensed practical nurse course that would begin in the fall. Then in September, I met Marilyn again in the soup kitchen. She had come in to ask Christine for a safety pin, since her pants were falling down. It was then that I noticed how much weight Marilyn had lost. Christine produced a diaper pin and asked Marilyn if she had been sleeping in her (nonfunctioning) car. Marilyn said yes.

There had been a fire in the apartment building in which she lived. The town had put Marilyn up at the local motel, a mile outside of Middle City. On Sunday morning, the motel owner had ordered Marilyn to be out of the room in ten minutes. He was angry that the town had not yet paid him the rent money. At this point, the only place Marilyn could think of to go was her car, which was still parked in her previous landlord's driveway.

After being evicted from the motel, Marilyn became totally demoralized. She did not go back to the town to ask for more housing. The precipitating event for her homelessness was an eviction, and subsequently she gave up hope of finding housing. I noticed during our hours together that day that Marilyn had a musty odor about her. Previously, Marilyn had prided herself on keeping clean. Marilyn's decision not to pursue more housing is similar to the path taken by many homeless people (Baxter and Hopper 1981).

At this point, Marilyn's thoughts were a jumble of plans. She said:

> Irene, I looked into trips to Europe. If I took a boat trip to Europe, I would have housing for thirteen days. Then, once I got there, maybe they would have a better welfare system than is here. If I took a plane, it would only be a couple of hours' ride. I'd prefer the boat.

For several hours, I worked hard at trying to locate a shelter that would take Marilyn. The closest one was in her hometown. She refused to go. She ended up agreeing to go to a shelter in Western City. Shelter rules required that one show up, in person, by five o'clock and leave by seven the next morning; the stay was a maximum of twenty-one days. By the time arrangements had been made, it was too late for Marilyn to arrive by five, so she spent another night in the car. Marilyn did go to the shelter the next day and did not come back to Tabernacle Soup Kitchen after that. Viewed from Marilyn's point of view, it took tremendous amounts of her already depleted mental and physical energies to make the move to Western City, and I could see why sleeping in a car would seem better than an unknown and quite probably hostile environment she might enter.

Pedro: In Search of Tranquilidad

Pedro, the portly fifty-five-year-old Puerto Rican man mentioned in Chapter 4, was one of my key informants for two and a half years, perhaps because we were best able to have a reciprocal relationship. He could communicate with me in Spanish and thereby have an interested listening ear and an advocate. For my part, I could know a person who was inside the soup kitchen community and could present me with the world view of a soup kitchen guest.

During the first year of our relationship, Pedro was one of the workfare kitchen crew, though he also spent his days off in there. In 1984 he developed a severe rash on his hands, and the dermatologist said he could no longer work. He was then diagnosed as having cancer in his lower back. He was treated as an outpatient at a hospital in a neighboring town, and he spent all of his mornings in the soup kitchen.

Pedro was a member of two communities: the soup kitchen and the Hotel Paradise. When he was not in the soup kitchen, he was often standing outside the doors of the hotel, greeting people he knew as they walked by. Most of the men who stood in front of the hotel from morning until night appeared drunk or high on drugs, but Pedro appeared to be sober. He told me that he had a former wife in Puerto Rico, and that he had two grown daughters, one in Spain and one in New York City. One day Pedro showed me his room, which was cramped and dark. His drawers were filled with correspondence from various organizations promising that he would be the winner of a color television set if he sent back a crossword puzzle game, or that he could purchase a miracle from a golden Buddha living in the Himalayan Mountains. The letters were in English, and Pedro seemed to have understood some of them, with the help of the pictures of dollar bills that covered the letters.

Pedro had moved from the western part of the state three years before; in his life there, he may have had more personal relationships. He told me that he had a brother in the former town, and that he had worked for a Cuban bakery (though the job may have been, like his job at the soup kitchen, "supported work"). A trophy on his bureau attested to his involvement in a domino tournament. It was not clear why Pedro had moved to Middle City. The two reasons most of the Puerto Rican population of the soup kitchen gave were the *tranquilidad* and their wish to get away from some "trouble" in another town.

At the soup kitchen, Pedro greeted the other Puerto Rican men, joked with the young women who lived at the hotel, and was Popi (the affectionate Spanish term for father) to the toddlers of the soup kitchen, whom he would pick up and hug. Pedro was one of the people of the soup kitchen who would appear, at first glance, to be able to hold down a job in the competitive market. But as I got to know Pedro, I wondered if he really would be able to obtain a job.

I heard him speak in simple sentences in English, and he appeared
to understand the other kitchen workers. When asked, however, if
he spoke English (as he would be by a prospective employer), he
would say that he did not.

In the winter of 1985 Pedro had severe back pain which was
diagnosed as cancer. He spent the next year and a half in and out of
the hospital for surgery and radiation therapy. When he was in
Middle City, he continued his daily walk (now with a cane) to the
soup kitchen, and continued to watch the world from the sidewalk

in front of the Hotel Paradise. In the summer of 1986 he died in a nursing home. His memorial service was held in the chapel above the soup kitchen. Ten friends and several social workers came. A fund was set aside by the soup kitchen in Pedro's memory, and a child's play sink and stove were purchased for the children's area.

Lives of Chronic Loneliness

Jane: A Life of Disabilities

Every day at noon Jane walked over from her sheltered workshop to eat and socialize in the soup kitchen. Jane was a woman in her fifties, who walked with a stiff, unbalanced gait and spoke in a labored manner in sentences that often ended with a nervous laugh. She also cried easily during conversation, especially when speaking of the recent theft of her TV set, or in worrying whether her rent would be raised. Her hair was graying and most of the time was wild looking, standing out around her head in all directions. At times when I was with Jane, I noticed the smell of stale urine about her. At first glance, she appeared to be retarded. However, after observing her for over two years at the soup kitchen, I doubted that she was retarded. She had been an organizer for the handicapped in the state, and one day she brought in her album filled with newspaper clippings about herself, as well as her correspondence with various state officials. In these letters she had described herself as "motor impaired." She could read and write, and her vocabulary was at times surprising. One day she asked me if I had sent her regards to a fellow anthropologist who used to be acquainted with Jane through the state's handicapped network. When I said I had, she asked me, "Well, was Alice responsive?"

Jane had a few friends in the soup kitchen, including another woman in her fifties and, before his death, George. Jane told me about her life, which she herself described as lonely. She lived with her mother all of her life, until her mother had died a slow, painful death from cancer several years before. Jane described her mother as having become "crazy" during that time. Jane tried seeking help from the local mental health clinic, but she said that there was no help because they would not make house calls. She often referred to her mother, in tears, and spoke fondly of her. Christine, the soup kitchen director, told me that she believed that Jane's mother was extremely protective of Jane all her life, and that this was why she gave the appearance of being less capable than she really was.

In an effort to understand more about Jane's life outside the soup kitchen, I asked her if she would give me a tour of her sheltered workshop. She said that she would love to. I arrived at a cavernous, partially abandoned factory about a mile and a half from her house (she walked there each day). The receptionist of the sheltered workshop led me into a huge, barren-looking room that could have been a scene out of Charles Dickens. Someone bellowed out Jane's name, and she and the shop supervisor came over to meet me. There were about fifty people in the workshop that day, all of whom were retarded or had severe physical handicaps. Most of the people wore their overcoats, though the room did not feel especially cold. Jane did piecework at the workshop for three hours a day, five days a week. That day she seemed eager to leave the shop early and go with me back to the soup kitchen.

Jane was a good example of someone who had discovered a variety of ways to cope with life on a limited income (she received Social Security disability payments) and with physical and mental disabilities. In addition to the workshop, she baby-sat for school-age children in the evening. On Sundays she went to church. She occasionally mentioned to me that the priest asked people to pray that the local welfare authorities would find it in their hearts to give poor people money. Although I didn't see people gravitating to Jane, she looked as though she was eager for conversation. She was a good observer of people around her, and she would comment to me about who was looking better these days and who was looking worse.

Beth: A Lonely Life

I started to notice Beth in the spring of 1985 (see Chapter 4). She was a woman in her early fifties who usually sat alone at a center table. She had graying, rather wild-looking hair, and was often dressed in a kitchen worker's uniform. She was friendly when I greeted her, but at that time I could learn no more from her than that she worked part-time, lived alone, and enjoyed coming to the soup kitchen.

In the fall of 1985, Beth became one of the members of the community counseling class at the soup kitchen. She told us over the weeks of the course that she grew up in one of the rural towns near Middle City and had to leave school in the eighth grade to go to work. She said that her mother abused her and her sister, and that she always admired the adopted children in her class because they seemed to have so much more than she had. She had been married and divorced and had one grown daughter whom she rarely saw.

Beth spoke of her mother, who had died of cancer. Since her mother's death, she seemed to have led a very isolated life. She worked for three or four hours a day, and then went back to her small apartment. She spent her mornings in the soup kitchen, drinking coffee and speaking to no one. Once the community counseling class began and she was introduced to some of the other guests, she talked in the group about her childhood, her mother, and her current drinking, which she said was out of control. Although she had been married, she gave the impression of a person with few friends throughout her life. Most of the time in the soup kitchen, she looked as though she were sitting and waiting for someone to take the initiative to be sociable toward her.

Esther: A Soup Kitchen Regular

Esther was another soup kitchen regular. As described in Chapter 4, she was a woman in her fifties who walked with a limp as a result of severe chronic arthritis brought about by congenital hip problems. She arrived each morning by way of Dial-a-Ride, the publicly subsidized van for the elderly and disabled, from her apartment in a local housing project. She sat at the table nearest the kitchen with a group of women in their forties and fifties. She was divorced and had two sons, aged eighteen and twenty. Her eighteen-year-old had recently graduated from the special education class of the local high school.

Esther told me that her parents would not take care of her when she was born. Her first few years were spent in a hospital for crippled children in the state. She was then brought up by foster parents. Her life appeared to have been punctuated by physical problems and hospitalizations.

Esther may have been somewhat unusual in the soup kitchen in that she was affiliated with the Cub Scouts, which is a more formal social group than most of the guests typically have contact with. She helped at their meetings and fund raisers. She often sat at the table in the soup kitchen crocheting afghans for Cub Scout fairs. In the spring, she wore a jacket which had Cub Scout patches sewn on practically every inch of material. She joked that the jacket was held together by the patches. She also commented in all seriousness that she would never get rid of it.

Esther was also one of the small group of people the director occasionally recruited for jobs—for example, addressing the church's newsletter to volunteers and community supporters of the soup kitchen, or doing some typing. She was a high school graduate and had worked for many years as a counter waitress at the local Woolworth's five and dime store. She said that she could not find another job once the store went out of business. She appeared to feel comfortable in the soup kitchen in the company of other women who would sit there for two or three hours discussing their lives. On the morning after her son's graduation from high school, Esther, who I believe was feeling especially nostalgic, brought in her portable stereo and played tapes of songs sung by Johnny Mathis. These songs of the 1950s and 1960s suggested an era in her life when she felt more promise for the future.

Summary

Some of the guests, like Marilyn and Sue, had clearly identifiable losses, such as loss of physical and mental health, loss of family, and loss of income, and were driven to the soup kitchen hoping it might provide some comfort in their lives. Other guests might not have suffered such recent dramatic losses, though their lives clearly put them outside of the "highly competitive cornucopian socioeconomic system" (Baxter and Hopper 1981: ii) of the larger society: Pedro lived on general assistance in the local hotel; Ralph had a history of prison; Jane had lived with her physical and mental problems all of her life; Beth had few friends and family; and Esther's physical disabilities and inability to work limited her social life.

The life circumstances of all had made their existence lonely and brought them to the soup kitchen in search of sociability. Once they found the soup kitchen, they became regulars. And even when they left town, as in the case of Marilyn, they probably sought out another soup kitchen in order to find social relationships.

The director of the Tabernacle Soup Kitchen, and other directors with whom I have spoken, appear to realize that the greetings of the people who serve the food as the guest walks past the serving line, plate in hand, may be the guests' only friendly words of the day. During their time of regular use, I believe that the Tabernacle Soup Kitchen became of central focus for Sue, Pat, Ralph, Pedro, Marilyn, Jane, Beth, and Esther.

There is a small but growing social science literature on the importance of public spaces in the lives of the urban poor. The search for sociability has been documented in laundromats (Kenen 1982), secondhand clothing stores (Wiseman 1979), on the streets, and in train stations and rest rooms (Baxter and Hopper 1981). In fact, the desire for companionship is characteristic of the homeless population reported on by Baxter and Hopper. They noted that despite the nomadic existence of the homeless in New York City, most were eager to talk to the researchers, sought out the most populous places to keep warm, and directly expressed their loneliness and desire for social interaction. The soup kitchen offers one more setting for social interaction in contemporary life.

7

An Ambience of Acceptance

In addition to the general sociability found within the dining room, guests of the Tabernacle Soup Kitchen find a haven of acceptance for themselves that contrasts sharply with the aversion with which they are viewed by much of the rest of society. This chapter is devoted to exploring the atmosphere of acceptance and its impact on individual soup kitchen guests.

Almost all of the guests of the Tabernacle Soup Kitchen may be defined as deviant from the mainstream of contemporary society. *Deviance* is generally defined as behavior that violates the norms of a society. For example, adults are normally employed or otherwise "productively" engaged in daily work. By that standard, the majority of the 80 to 100 people who gather in the Tabernacle Soup Kitchen each morning would be considered deviant. In addition, some of the guests may violate certain unspoken expectations for public behavior by, for example, audibly laughing and talking to themselves, or pacing the floor. Some have physical disabilities that mark them as different from the norms of physical health. Many have been publicly labeled as deviant by having had a psychiatric hospitalization or a criminal involvement. The majority (81 percent) described themselves as suffering from depression, nervousness, illegal drug use, alcoholism, or suicidal thoughts or attempts when asked about mental health issues in the community health survey in the fall of 1983.

In 1982 the author/journalist Susan Sheehan vividly described the life of a chronically mentally ill young woman named Sylvia Frumpkin, whose constant lament to the author and to the rest of society was, "Is there no place on earth for me?" (Sheehan 1982). The soup kitchen appears to be one place on earth for the mentally ill and others who are different from the rest of society in negatively viewed ways. The soup kitchen offers its guests several hours of warmth, nourishment, sociability, and acceptance.

I will suggest in this chapter that the soup kitchen is able to provide asylum in the original meaning of "a place of sanctuary" (*Webster's New Riverside Dictionary* II 1984: 45) for many people who deviate from public norms of behavior. The guests for whom the soup kitchen provides refuge are those who are chronically mentally ill or physically disabled, or who violate the law. This amalgam is often referred to as "street people" (Bachrach 1984), because of all the time they spend on the streets and in other public places.

As I came to know the guests of the Tabernacle Soup Kitchen, I found that almost all, whatever else they were facing in life, had behaviors that could have been categorized as "mental health problems" by the psychiatric system. It may be hypothesized that these behaviors were both a contributing factor and a *result* of their daily struggle for survival. What was outstanding in the soup kitchen was not the *diagnosability* of the guests in mental health terms, but the atmosphere of acceptance of each other that prevailed among the guests. The very mission of the Tabernacle Soup Kitchen to "offer a trustful community resource for the poor, providing safe harbor, social contract, information and referral, and moral support to its easily defeated clientele" (brochure of the Tabernacle Soup Kitchen) avoids the urge to reform, treat, or judge, and promotes the atmosphere of acceptance.

In a different era, those with chronic mental illness would have been committed to psychiatric facilities. Since the 1950s, however, public psychiatric hospitals have shortened stays for inpatients, and admission standards have become more stringent. The result has been the process of *deinstitutionalization*. The pressures leading to this massive effort were the apparent ineffectiveness of long-term hospitalization, widespread use of psychotropic drugs that appear to control the symptoms of the major psychoses, and increased costs of hospitalization (Rousseau 1981). Deinstitutionalization has forced many mentally ill people into the "community": often to their hometowns or to the area nearest the psychiatric hospital, which typically has few resources to deal with the discharged patients. The dearth of services and activities for the mentally ill is one of the contributing factors in the growing problem of homelessness in the United States (Lamb 1984; Bachrach 1984).

In examining the ambiance of acceptance in the soup kitchen, it is helpful to consider the examples of those guests whose "deviance" manifests itself in a variety of ways. Each person I will describe below has found his way to the soup kitchen and is there *voluntarily* for several hours at a time. This contrasts with the experience of the mental health system where the person with chronic mental illness is considered hard to reach and presently is considered a drain on the system because of missed or canceled appointments.

Finding Asylum: Mental Health Issues

Mark: Alone and Pacing

Mark was a thin young man in his twenties whose face perpetually wore an intense frown. His two outstanding features were his clothes and his relentless pacing. His clothes were often inappropriate for the weather conditions. For example, on hot days he often dressed in oversized shoes, pants many sizes too big for him, and a large hooded sweatshirt which he wore with the hood wrapped tightly around his head. On the other hand, he often wore only pants and a tee shirt on the coldest days of winter, and I would see him walking quickly from one side of town to another.

I started to notice Mark in Middle City several years before my work began in the soup kitchen, and I had noticed what seemed to me to be his quick walk away from people. I was interested to see that he was able to tolerate the human contact inside the dining room of the soup kitchen. He seemed to speak to no one and often paced the floor with his plate filled with food. Occasionally the director would suggest to him that he sit down with his food, which he eventually did, choosing a seat far away from the others.

Mark also frequented the community action program's storefront office. They accepted his coming in and out, his drinking coffee, and his sitting on the radiator to keep warm. Kate, the sympathetic director of the agency, told me that Mark had a long history of psychiatric hospitalizations, but that every time she mentioned the mental health clinic or a counselor to him he ran out of the office. Kate considered it progress for Mark to want to come to the soup kitchen.

Steve: Laughing to Himself

Steve was a young man about 6'5" tall, extremely thin, disheveled, and dirty, with long blond hair. Daily he rode his bicycle to the soup kitchen, where he could often be seen talking and laughing to himself. I knew of Steve when he was a resident at a halfway house for former psychiatric patients. After several months in the program, he was asked to leave for disobeying the rules. Most of the staff thought he would not survive by himself in the community, but in fact, though still laughing and talking to himself, he blended in well at the soup kitchen.

One day Steve told me that he was worried about the babies drowning, and about being electrocuted by the open electrical circuits all over the soup kitchen (drowning babies and open circuits appeared to be visible only to Steve). He often sat with Carl, a man in his forties who told me that he too had many mental problems, and when I approached Carl he was often also muttering and laughing to himself. He seemed to have befriended Steve, and in the soup kitchen, when they sat together, Carl would tell Steve when his laughing was disturbing others.

Madeline: Walking in Traffic

Madeline was the tall woman in her twenties, with long black hair, who lived at the "thieves' den" (Chapter 4). When I first began conversing with her, she was a worker on the general assistance workfare kitchen crew. At first Madeline was fairly communicative and typically she would say to me,

> Irene, I want my daughter back. The state took her from me when I was in Greenville hospital. Now I want her back. I'm not taking my medication because I don't like to, and I don't need to talk to the psychiatrist at the mental health clinic. My only problem is that I'm too fat. I'm a pig. Sometimes, when I feel beautiful I look at my hands. Irene, can you find me a job? I like your earrings—you look nice today.

I gave Madeline some suggestions about finding a job and helped her set up an appointment with a labor department program. She went, but was very discouraged and wouldn't go back because, she said, they didn't have a job for her right away.

Over the next six months, Madeline became more and more disoriented. I often saw her walking quickly through the streets, in and out of traffic, muttering to herself. She had in her hands a rock magazine, black with dirt. I noticed that she had the magazine with her continuously in the streets and in the soup kitchen. She still greeted me; she still said that I "looked nice," and she'd ask me for money. She went in and out of bakeries and grocery stores, asking for food. She walked in such a frantic way, I wondered how she managed to avoid getting hit by a car. Christine asked the outreach social worker to see her, but Madeline ran out of the soup kitchen when she saw her coming. After about six months, Madeline was committed to the state hospital again.

Hector and Las Brujas

Hector was a Puerto Rican man in his forties, with few teeth in his mouth; he was a guest and a workfare kitchen worker. I became acquainted with him in the fall of 1983, when he was working in the kitchen. He told me that he had gotten into some kind of legal difficulty in Western City, was on probation, and had come to Middle City to be alone and stay out of trouble. Hector lived in the Hotel Paradise, and he seemed to have few social relationships. After he realized that he could communicate with me in Spanish, he told me that *las brujas* (the witches) were after him. He told me that this had been going on since he was sixteen, and that his wife and children in Puerto Rico were hexing him more and more. I asked him if he had received letters from them, and he said no. The soup kitchen nurse told me that she thought he might be having delirium tremens, and that these were his hallucinations. One day when Hector was especially distraught, I called a Puerto Rican social worker at the mental health clinic. He told Hector, over the phone, to come up to see him at the clinic in two weeks. Hector never went and soon after that he left Middle City.

In the fall of 1985 I again met Hector. He told me that he had tried to live in Western City and was returning to Middle City for the *tranquilidad*. He appeared thinner, but essentially the same. During this period of our conversations, he no longer talked about witches, but said that he got "drunk to be happy." He also told me he knew that he shouldn't drink. When I greeted him in the dining room (he was usually standing close to the coffeepot), he would start to take various little pieces of papers and appointment cards out of his pocket for my translation into Spanish. I felt quite certain that he knew what the papers said, but perhaps he wanted me to stop and talk.

One day, when I had not been in the dining room, I saw Hector on the street, leaving the soup kitchen with the help of two other Puerto Rican men. Hector was so drunk that he was falling down. He was yelling at his friends to leave him alone. Finally, they let him sit on the sidewalk.

Although I do not know specifically that he had been in a psychiatric hospital, his mental health and drinking problems were obvious. Hector was able to find some moments of camaraderie and acceptance in the soup kitchen each day, despite his troubles.

Butch: People Are After Me

I had known Butch by sight for two years before he talked to me. He was a short man in his forties, and most often sat alone. He always seemed to be smiling, and when I greeted him he muttered something about wanting to see a former counselor at the mental health clinic. One day, two years after I had first seen him, he came over and said to me in a great rush of words:

> Hello, isn't your name Fran? No? It's Irene, then hello. I want to make an effort to get to know more people. I used to be a barber, but I haven't worked in years—you know—people are after me.

As we continued talking, he gave me examples of how people were after him.

> One day I was walking down the street and I said hi to an old friend from high school. I hadn't seen him for a long time, and when he stopped to say hello, he went and broke my glasses. (shows me the broken rim). Another time I was driving home at night, and I pulled over to the side of the road on Main Street. I was just sitting there, thinking how I could get some water for my car to get it going again. Then some c.b.'ers came along and asked me if I needed help. I said no, but they came back fifteen minutes later and asked again. This time when I said no, they called the police, who had me committed to Greenville. After fifteen days, I was released and had to pay $100 for storing my car!

Toward the end of our conversation, Butch told me that he hoped to have an interview at a program that had apartments for people with chronic mental illness.

Finding Asylum: Physically Handicapped

Mike: Lying Down

Mike was a college graduate with a degree in engineering. He had a back problem which required him to spend most of his time lying down. He was assigned to the soup kitchen through workfare, and was often lying on an uncovered, dirty, foam rubber mattress, whether he was playing with the toddlers (one of his soup kitchen jobs) or eating his dinner. He told me that his back problem was congenital and incurable. He said that he was eager to work, if a company would accept his working lying down. Mike told me repeatedly that the only thing stopping him from working was the prejudice and discrimination that most engineering companies had against the idea of a person working at home lying down. After he had been at the soup kitchen for a week, I noticed that nobody looked twice at his supine position, and the children told me that they looked forward to his time with them.

Mike was a worker in the soup kitchen for over a year. During this time, he established the job of maintaining the bulletin board, which listed apartments for rent and job openings. Although the job did not require a degree in engineering, it did require literacy. The bulletin board was a success in terms of its usefulness to other guests, and it enabled Mike to work lying down. In the meantime, he continued to go to pain clinics for his back problem, and to scour the employment ads for a job outside the soup kitchen that he could do in a supine position.

Andy: A Scarred Face

Andy, in his early twenties, was a soup kitchen regular throughout the spring of 1983. He had been in a car accident that left the side of his face badly scarred and one of his eyes almost entirely closed. He told me that he was very nervous, and he chain smoked and was always moving in his chair. He told me that he had recently been rejected by his girl friend, and he spent hours in the soup kitchen telling and retelling his plight to anyone who would listen. He said that when he woke up each morning and saw himself in the mirror, he almost scared himself.

Andy seemed to be well liked by a group of other young men in the soup kitchen. One day, when the piano had been unlocked, he got up from the table, sat down, and played Debussy's "Clair de Lune." This suggested to me that Andy's childhood may have been more organized and more affluent than his current life. He said that his dream was to be a great rock star.

Finding Asylum: In Trouble with the Law

Ismael: On His Way to Jail

A number of the guests of the Tabernacle Soup Kitchen had recently been in jail, were awaiting a trial date, or were currently engaged in breaking the law. They too found asylum and acceptance in the soup kitchen. The situation of Ismael illustrates the degree of acceptance a person could find there.

I met Ismael in the fall of 1985 when he was on the workfare program in the kitchen crew. He also became a member of the class on community counseling. Ismael, in his thirties, was about twenty pounds overweight, and often was sweating. He was bilingual in English and Spanish and spoke both languages in a nervous, rushed manner. He had come to Middle City from New York City, in hopes of "staying out of trouble."

Ismael told the group in the community counseling class that he had been severely abused as a child. He said that his father always hated him and had tried to kill him several times, once by shoving him out of a window and another time by putting his head in an oven. Much of the time, I got the impression that Ismael was high on drugs—he would be agitated and sweating, and his eyes would look dazed. One day as I was walking on Main Street in Middle City, I heard a man singing at the top of his lungs. I looked over and saw Ismael. He smiled and said that he was singing because he was happy. I thought that if there had been a policeman around, Ismael would have been questioned and probably searched for drugs.

After several months in the soup kitchen, Ismael was arrested on charges of possession of drug paraphernalia, possession of marijuana, and larceny—stealing and using credit cards. One day he came to the soup kitchen after spending the night in jail. He showed a group of us in the dining room all of his paper work from court. He was adamant that he was innocent, claiming that he found the credit cards under the rug of his room at the Hotel Paradise, and that they could have been there for years. He said that the cigarette was filled with tobacco, not marijuana. Finally, he said that he needed the needles and syringes the police had found in his room for his skin allergies. He received a lot of support from the other guests, who said that he was innocent.

Two weeks after the charges, Ismael was admitted to a twenty-eight-day program for alcoholics. His friends told me that he really needed help. Soon after his hospitalization, he went to jail.

Welcome Back to the Soup Kitchen

The accepting philosophy of the soup kitchen also means that even when people return to the dining room after an absence of several months they are warmly greeted. I saw this illustrated in the case of Marilyn.

The last time I had seen Marilyn was when I had said good bye to her as she was on her way to Western City to try to find an apartment and work toward having her children returned to her. One year later, as I was walking down the stairs of the soup kitchen, I saw the back of a woman with long gray hair, a slender physique, and suitcases by her side. I immediately recognized Marilyn.

After I greeted her, she told me that in the year since we had seen each other she had lived in at least four shelters throughout the state. Finally, she had gotten a room in a hotel in Western City. It was not an apartment, and she still could not cook in her room, but she at least felt a bit safer than she had in her months of sleeping in shelters.

Marilyn was back in town for a court hearing regarding her children. The state was petitioning to have her relinquish her parental rights, which would make the children eligible for adoption. Her suitcases were filled with papers and pictures that showed (she hoped) that she had not abandoned her children and should not have her children permanently removed from her. She was in the soup kitchen to warm up, get a cup of coffee and a meal, and wait for her court appearance.

Christine welcomed Marilyn back. She said, "I'm glad you could join us for lunch." In the several hours Marilyn stayed in Middle

City, she lost her bus ticket back to Western City. Christine let her leave her suitcases with her (Christine's office contains other personal belongings of people who have left them with her for "several hours") while Marilyn and I searched for her ticket. I believe that, if we had not found it, Christine would have given Marilyn money for another one.

Marilyn was able to use the Tabernacle Soup Kitchen as her home base while in Middle City, where she stayed for five hours. The court ordered several more months of investigation, and I saw her off at the bus station.

Smoking in the Soup Kitchen

The attitude of acceptance in the soup kitchen is also exemplified by the policy on cigarette smoking. Although quantitative data on the number of smokers are not available, it is clear that by 11 A.M. the dining room itself smells from the widespread smoking. The City Ministry Committee and the soup kitchen director, Christine, have been asked numerous times why smoking is permitted. The critics (many of whom I assume donate food and money) say that since smoking is an unhealthful habit, the soup kitchen should not permit it. Further, they say that if the guests are poor, they should not be spending their money on cigarettes.

To these arguments, Christine (a nonsmoker) explains that smoking is a part of the life-style of many of the guests. Forbidding it would be a rejection of the guests and would seriously diminish the accepting ambiance of the soup kitchen. To at least partially resolve the issue, an anonymous donor gave an air filter, which was somewhat helpful in keeping the air in the dining room fresh, despite the pervasive smoking.

The Soup Kitchen: A Problem-Free Service

The accepting ambiance of the soup kitchen exists because the service itself exerts almost no demands on the guests. The kind of service that has no eligibility requirements, keeps no records, and makes no demands on its clientele has been called "problem-free" (Rousseau 1981)—an interesting shift in terminology, since in the mental health field the "problem" is usually viewed as residing in the client and not in the agency. The Tabernacle Soup Kitchen's only requirements are that the guest not drink or use drugs while there (though a guest may be high) and that there be no violence.

The guests of the soup kitchen do much to create the uncritical atmosphere. They include everyone at a table in the general conversation. They do not stare at people who may be pacing, laughing, or talking to themselves. For example, one day, in her state of disorientation, Madeline accidentally spilled her soup on Sue, the young woman recovering from an almost fatal mugging. Although at first Sue thought that Madeline had done it on purpose, the rest of the people at the table assured her that it had been an accident, allowing for Madeline's mistake. Had Madeline not been so obviously disturbed at this point, the incident might have led to a verbal, if not a physical, fight.

One might hypothesize that the guests themselves do not notice the behaviors around them, but I feel that they do notice. For example, one day, as I was sitting at a crowded table nearest the coffeepot, a tall man, whom the director had previously described to me as "practically catatonic," came over and sat down. I had never, in the seven months of seeing him, heard him talk. He carried on a conversation with another man at the table, who was a regular member of the social group made up of residents of the hotel. The "practically catatonic" man, with a French Canadian accent, talked about how he would never become a U.S. citizen. After he had left, the first man addressed the entire table.

> After I got out of Greenville [state psychiatric hospital] I come down here to the soup kitchen and what do I find—the same nuts I knew up there!

In many ways, the soup kitchen encompasses the accepting, low-key, survival-oriented programs that are suggested for people with chronic mental health problems (Appleby, Slagg, and Desai 1982). In a discussion of vagrancy and psychosis in third-world countries (Baasher et al. 1983), the authors suggest that the developing countries have an opportunity to establish the kind of services that will be effective for the homeless mentally ill, rather than imitating the organized, bureaucratic welfare system of the developed countries. They suggest that *contact facilities*, a term used by Leach (1979) to describe night shelters and soup runs (kitchens), may be advisable for those expressing no desire for help or interaction. The soup kitchen is in many ways reminiscent of the ambiance of acceptance of deviance of the town of Gheel, Belgium, which, since the fifteenth century, has been offering homes to the chronically mentally ill (Hombs and Snyder 1972).

The soup kitchen, in its attitude toward various differences, may also be compared with the Italian Democratic Psychiatry Movement conceptualized in the work and writings of Franco Basaglia (Lovell 1978; Scheper-Hughes 1983). This movement addresses the social class and power issues inherent in traditional psychiatry. The movement has successfully opened up the mental hospitals of Gorizia and Trieste, Italy, by helping the former patients with issues of economic survival, and by restoring their identity as people instead of patients. It is interesting to note that a new legal category has been created for the former patients—that of *ospite*, which is guest in Italian. The status was created in part to give the people a subsidy.

In a sociological analysis tracing the path toward deviance, Dinitz, Dynes, and Clarke (1975) suggest that the individual first engages in some behavior that is different and defined as undesirable; then he is accorded low status within the society; the person accepts the negative evaluation of others and devalues himself; and finally, this "spoiled identity" makes it difficult to have social relationships, so there begins a period of social isolation. The soup kitchen community challenges the inevitability of social isolation by offering a place of tolerance, if not acceptance, for the "deviant." The kinds of deviance found in the soup kitchen—whether the mental illness of Mark, Steve, Madeline, Hector, and Butch, the physical disability of Mike and Andy, the criminal charges against Ismael, or the wanderings of

Marilyn—are violations of ideal norms. One might hypothesize that the soup kitchen guest is not actually behaving more deviantly than others (other people have mental and physical disabilities, and have committed criminal acts though few may be charged with the acts), but that there is more public acknowledgment of the differences.

This lack of negative judgments of deviance seems to embody the goal of cultural relativism, of viewing differences as differences rather than as better or worse, moral or immoral (Kaplan and Manners 1972). Perhaps because every guest has his own life history ("his story") filled with deviations from the ideal, he is more tolerant of the differences of others. The underground world of the soup kitchen community might therefore hold important insights for the rest of society.

8

Social Networks and Social Support

As the last two chapters have shown, the dining room of the soup kitchen provides an atmosphere of sociability for the lonely and acceptance for the rejected. For some, however, the soup kitchen goes beyond these functions and offers its guests the opportunity to affiliate with each other and form social relationships. These relationships develop in part because there is a fairly predictable structure, as people become accustomed to sitting at particular tables, with particular individuals with whom they feel comfortable. Human interaction and social togetherness appear to flourish in the relatively peaceful, nonthreatening, quasi-structured surroundings of the dining room. Here is a time and place to establish or renew social ties. These social ties, or social networks, can be seen daily within the Tabernacle Soup Kitchen.

We can examine the social networks that exist within the soup kitchen by a visual mapping of the dining room, in which tables tend to be dominated by loosely knit friendship groups. Each day, as people enter the soup kitchen, they gravitate to their table of friends and acquaintances. The tables themselves also tend to stay constant with, for example, the women and children gathering in the area with a broken crib and dirty rug that is farthest from the kitchen, the middle-aged women gathering closest to the kitchen, and the hotel men gathering closest to the coffeepot and near the door. I would suggest that the women feel safest with their children away from the activity of the kitchen, the middle-aged women feel most comfortable identifying with the kitchen crew that prepares the meal, and the hotel men like to be close to the door for a quick exit when needed. In addition to the tables full of people are the individuals who are a part of several social networks that "float" among the tables. It is as though they resist being "trapped" at a tableful of people.

The following map shows the dining room at approximately 11 A.M., when about one-third to one-half of the guests have arrived. The social networks tend to be most obvious at this time, since people who come to the soup kitchen this early (the meal isn't served until 12:30) appear to be there for social reasons.

Beyond the observation and mapping of social networks is the perhaps more important question of how these relationships are perceived. In other words, how *supportive* are these social networks?

Social support is an important concept because of the buffering effects it has been found to have on a large group of physical, mental, and environmental stresses in life (Schaefer, Coyne, and Lazarus 1981: 382). However, one of the problems of social science research regarding social support is that too often social networks and social support are discussed as though they are synonymous and interchangeable. The problem then is that many benefits that have been found to emanate from social support are thought to exist when one observes people affiliating with each other on a regular basis (see Schaefer, Coyne, and Lazarus 1981 for a good discussion of the distinction between social networks and social support).

Social support may be emotional, tangible, and informational.

Emotional support includes intimacy and attachment, reassurance, and being able to confide in and rely on another—all of which contribute to the feeling that one is loved or cared about, or even that one is a member of a group, not a stranger. *Tangible* support involves direct aid or services and can include loans, gifts of money or goods, and provision of services such as taking care

Table 8.1
Map of the Tabernacle Soup Kitchen at 11 A.M.

Enter

Children's corner

                                                                old
Gamache extended fam. (9)   Alan and Bob   refrig.

Single man, talking   5 teen-age boys

2 women, 3 children

Single father, 2 children   Sue's group (5 women)

6 men   Single woman

          Marcos
          (standing)   Peggy's table (10)

Pedro's table (8 hotel men)
                                   Serving table
          Barbara
          (standing)

     Coffeepot

Enter   Kitchen

Men's bathroom

Second
floor—Women's bathroom

of needy persons or doing a chore for them. *Informational* support includes giving information and advice which could help a person solve a problem. . . . Tangible and informational support may also serve an emotional support function, as when they signal caring and are not viewed as resulting from obligation. (Schaefer, Coyne, and Lazarus 1981: 385)

Faced with the challenge of assessing social support within the soup kitchen one must somehow enter the social networks for long enough and intimately enough to observe interactions which may be perceived as "supportive" by the participants. One model for doing this research with a similar group of people is provided by the study of social networking within single-room-occupancy hotels in New York City (Shapiro 1969). Through extensive participant observation, quasi-familiar groups were shown to be forming around central matriarchal figures. "Groups exist whose members give mutual support to each other's deviant or maladaptive behavior, but who also provide the human association, the sense of some help and belonging, which makes physical survival possible and emotional life meaningful" (Shapiro 1969: 646). Another qualitative analysis of social networking is presented in the study of homeless alcoholic men. These men were studied in a tavern over a six-month period in their relationship to the central figure of Pete, the tavern bartender (Dumont 1967).

The following are examples of social networks that appeared to offer their participants some degree of emotional, tangible, and informational support. As is the case with social networks anywhere, not all of the interaction was uniformly supportive, and I have tried to point out instances where the relationships did not provide comfort to the participants.

Peggy's Table

One of the largest social networks was the group that sat at what was known as Peggy's table. Peggy, in her early fifties, was approx-

imately 5'3" tall, weighed close to three hundred pounds, and had
no teeth. When I first met her she was a soup kitchen regular, often
loudly complaining about the food and discussing her own recipes.
Since the fall of 1983, Peggy was a workfare worker in the kitchen
and rapidly rose to the second in command after the director, Christine. When Christine was away, Peggy answered the phone, had the
keys to the pantries, and was looked to for guidance by the kitchen
crew.

Peggy sat at the head of the table of about ten women nearest to
the serving area of the dining room. She chain smoked cigarillos as
she talked to the women at her table. Often the conversation centered on the happenings of the previous evening. Most of the women
went to Henry's Place at night, a bar in the industrial section of
town. The owner, Henry, recently had been arrested on charges of
selling cocaine. The women discussed whom they saw the previous

night, and what they had to drink. They also used their morning talks to discuss their children, who were in trouble in school or the courts, or their landlord problems, or their complaints about the men in their lives. In this way they gave each other a chance to air their problems and provided themselves with some measure of emotional support.

One of the women who gathered around Peggy was Alice, a woman in her early thirties who looked at least ten years older. She had chronic neck and back problems and often wore a neck brace. She had no teeth, and in her conversations she often seemed to be crying. Alice lived with her husband and three school-age children. I noticed that she often looked to Peggy for advice, and usually did not sit at the table until Peggy was seated. For example, one morning at about 9:30 I noticed Alice sitting on some steps to the side of the dining room, her head leaning in her hands in a dejected manner. A few people were at Peggy's table, but Alice did not join them until Peggy herself was seated at the table. It was as though Peggy was Alice's main source of security in the group. Alice was a frail woman, especially in contrast to Peggy's stoutness, which heightened Peggy's protective role.

On another day, at about noon, while I sat at Peggy's table, Alice came in with her two daughters, ages seven and nine. She announced to the tableful of people that her daughters had been thrown out of school for having lice in their hair. She immediately received expressions of commiseration from the other women, who made comments such as "those god damn bastards at school." Peggy suggested that I accompany Alice and her daughters back to school to try to have the girls readmitted. We did this, and the school nurse agreed to have the girls back if their doctor said that what she was seeing in their hair were dead eggs and not lice. During this transaction I could see that Alice seemed to have a limited understanding of what was happening. She did not understand the instructions for removing the lice, and the nurse had lost patience explaining it to her. The nurse told me that the lice problem had been going on all year. Alice insisted that her problems with the school would soon be solved, since she was going to move to Colorado. She also said that she was waiting to hear from the state about her request to adopt a baby. Alice, the daughters, and I then walked back to the soup kitchen in time for lunch, and Alice reported to Peggy's table what had happened. The next week, the girls were allowed back in school.

Here we can see that Alice derived much emotional support in her plight against the school, and Peggy initiated an action (my advocacy) that might be of help to Alice. It is interesting to note that none of the women reacted with disgust to the thought of lice; their disgust was reserved for the school. Peggy offered Alice some informational support in her advice that I accompany her back to the school nurse.

Also at Peggy's table were Esther and Sara. Sara was a woman in her fifties, who also often wore a neck brace. She gave the impression of often being angry by punctuating her sentences with the adjective *friggin*. One day Peggy, Esther, and Sara were deeply embroiled in a conversation about a mutual friend who had, the previous night, become drunk and had called up each of the three women at about 3 A.M. The woman had then taken her young child in the car and driven around with her until 5 A.M., at which time she went to Peggy's apartment. The reaction of the three women to being called upon for help was interesting. On the one hand they said that they were exhausted and resentful because the woman "never took any advice anyway." On the other hand, the animation and length of their conversation seemed to indicate a high level of interest and enthusiasm for the incident. Both Esther and Sara looked at Peggy with respect for her judgment on the matter, since it was Peggy who eventually took the woman in.

Peggy also functioned as surrogate mother for some of the guests. Jim was an eighteen-year-old who lived with Peggy for a period of about three months in Middle City. He was a frail white-faced young man with deep-set eyes. He told me that he was constantly abused as a child, and that almost every bone in his body had been broken from abuse, accidents, or fights. Jim was severely beaten by some other youths in the parking lot behind the soup kitchen. He referred to Peggy as his foster mother and in the soup kitchen would refer to her as mom. During some point in their relationship, Peggy "threw him out" of her house, and the mother-son relation was over. Here we can see the limits of support. Jim, in fact, was a very needy young man, who probably needed the help of professionals.

In many ways the kind of respect and following Peggy commanded was similar to the characteristics of the dominant leaders in single-room-occupancy hotels (Shapiro 1969). The leaders within three different hotels were all women who themselves suffered from chronic health problems, were overweight, and were domineering. They were able to provide some of the other occupants of the hotels (their following) with material and emotional aid. The women were able to form an alliance with the professionals in the area hospitals and welfare offices, and became advocates for the hotel tenants whom they befriended.

Not all of the interaction that occurred at Peggy's table could be described as supportive. Betty, a tall good-looking woman in her thirties, was a member of the friendship group. She had two daughters, both of whom had been recently returned to her from foster care. Both of her previous husbands were Puerto Rican (Betty is not). She continuously complained about her daughters, and talked about how she had gotten angry with them before school. Her refrain was, "They are going to get it!"

At first Betty did not seem different from the other women at the table in her ability to give and receive support. However, over a period of time, I saw that she had a hard time listening or being sympathetic to the others. I first became aware of this when Pat came back to the soup kitchen after her six-year-old's death. Betty talked to Pat, in loud tones, about how surprised she was to see Pat's other children dressed up for the funeral. Whereas the other women at the table talked quietly, trying to reflect Pat's mood, Betty's voice was raised, and she acted as though nothing unusual had happened. On another day, as Faith, a young black woman with three children, was relating her problems with her landlord, Betty broke into the conversation to complain about "the Puerto Ricans and 'lezzies' [lesbians] upstairs." Betty went on in detail, talking about how the two women upstairs were having a fight and tried to choke each other in the hallway, as her children looked on. Later in the same morning, the two women of whom she spoke came to the soup kitchen and took a table at the opposite side of the dining room from Betty. Betty again started to talk loudly about "lezzies." I thought that she was trying to provoke a fight. On the other hand, I saw her give people rides in her car to places they needed to go, such as the welfare office twenty miles away.

Although Betty was a part of the social network at Peggy's table, she, like most people, was not always ready and able to give support. Similarly, in a study of the culture of homeless men, Dumont (1969) challenged the frequently repeated stereotype that bartenders give support and are a listening ear to the woes of their customers. As a matter of fact, after spending approximately six months in the tavern culture, Dumont discovered that the bartender, Pete, discouraged customers who tried to tell him their stories. Like the bartender, Betty may have been shutting out other people's problems as a self-protective device because she had enough problems in her own life.

Sue and Her Friends

Sue was the woman of twenty-four who had been a daily regular at the soup kitchen since the fall of 1983. She was hit on the head five years earlier, and was in a coma for two years. She was slowly recovering her physical equilibrium, her speech, and her memory. Recently, she had had a baby with a black man in his fifties. She was a resident of the SRO for most of time I knew her.

Sue attracted a group of friends around her, who came to her aid. At first she needed help with walking from the serving table to the dining room. Later, as her ability to walk improved, she needed the friendship and encouragement of the other young women of the hotel, since she frequently talked of how discouraged she was with her life. After she gave birth, her friends came to her aid, baby-sitting for several hours at a time, often at the soup kitchen. They formed a support group around her with a particular focus on helping her care for the baby.

One member of Sue's circle at the soup kitchen was Nancy. On some days Nancy dressed in a suit and looked as though she were a middle-class professional. On other days she wore old clothes and looked tense and tired. One day, I saw Nancy give Sue support and confrontation in a way that seemed to be especially effective. I was standing with them in the area between the working kitchen and the director's office. Nobody else was about, and Sue was again despondent, saying that her life was not worth living. To this, Nancy said, "Who out here could have survived what you did? Don't you have a man? Do you hug and kiss and all of that other good stuff?"

Sue's response was that nobody else out there in the dining room would have survived, and yes that she did have a boyfriend. Nancy's approach had been direct, challenging, and specific.

Another member of Sue's support network was Yolanda, a very pretty woman also in her twenties, and a resident of the hotel. Sue and Yolanda often sat at a table together at about 10 A.M., drank coffee, and smoked cigarettes. Sue often played solitaire while Yolanda knitted. One day, soon after Yolanda had had her third child (who, like the previous two, was taken away by the state and placed in foster care), Sue talked to me loudly and exuberantly about her own pregnancy. I could see that Yolanda was becoming more and more unhappy as Sue was happily telling about her doctor's appointment, her collection of baby clothes, and her application for welfare. It struck me that although Sue had Yolanda's support and sympathy most of the time, that at least on this day Sue was not reciprocating with an equal amount of sympathy.

After Sue had her baby in the summer of 1985, I would often see two other hotel women, Maureen (who herself was pregnant) and Ann, help Sue get the baby carriage down the steps to the dining room, help feed the baby her formula, and at times baby-sit for several hours at a time in the dining room. During this period in Sue's life she was complaining bitterly about her boyfriend, and she would occasionally come to the soup kitchen with a black eye from him. Her friends appeared proud to come to her rescue.

Sue was not the dominant leader in her group (as Peggy was), but she was able to make people come to her aid, offering her tangible and emotional support. Her friends also seemed to derive a certain amount of status from their helping and a sense of their own self-worth.

Alan and Bob: Help in Staying Sober

The relationship of Alan and Bob was a brief but intense friendship between two men in their twenties which developed and then flourished in the soup kitchen. It was an example of a strong sense of support between two people in the dining room.

Alan was from Middle City and was often employed on the second or third shift in janitorial jobs. (See Chapter 4.) He told me that as a child he was very sick, that he had a lot of problems in school. During one three-month period he was intensely involved with Bob, who was sometimes drunk in the soup kitchen. Whereas Alan told me that he always had a difficult time in school, Bob was a college graduate. He told me that during college, he worked as a bartender and this started his heavy drinking.

Both Bob and Alan were interested in "spreading the gospel" and were often in the soup kitchen together, reading the Bible. Both attended evening Bible study at a local Baptist church. When Bob was not in the soup kitchen, people often asked Alan where he was, and Alan seemed to be taking responsibility for Bob's well-being.

Bob was an intense young man, and when sober he talked about his dream of becoming a Baptist minister. However, there were many days when he showed up with a dreamy smile on his face, smelling of liquor. The two often sat at a table near a group of women and children. After three months Bob left town and Alan continued to be a guest of the soup kitchen, usually sitting with the women and children.

Pedro: Source of Stability for Hotel Men

From his seat near the coffee pot in the dining room, and his piece of sidewalk outside the Hotel Paradise, Pedro was a source of friendship and help to the other Puerto Rican men and women who came to Middle City. He let the newly arrived people know where to get welfare, food stamps, and clothes. He greeted people as they entered the dining room, and he was friendly with the soup kitchen volunteers.

Pedro also had several romantic relationships. He told me that his son Pedrocito was born in the summer of 1984 to a woman who lived in a local housing project. Another guest, Maureen, became pregnant with his child, although according to Maureen, he did not acknowledge this. I never saw them exchange a glance although they were often in the dining room at the same time.

Pedro had an affectionate relationship with many of the children in the soup kitchen. Sometimes, when one of the children was crying, he would walk over, pick up the crying child, and soothe him. Pedro was friends with Marie Gamache. When she entered the soup kitchen, he often greeted her with "Hey, let me buy you a cup of coffee and a donut." To this Marie laughed and said, "No, mucho gordo." She had learned some Spanish when she worked in a local poultry factory and she delighted in speaking to Pedro. Although I had never seen Pedro sit down and join the Gamache sisters and their children at the table, the friendship between Pedro and Marie seemed to allow him a supportive role with the young grandchildren.

Central Figures in the Soup Kitchen Dining Room

In addition to the central figures of the various social networks I have described, several people exerted an influence on many of the guests.

Barbara
Barbara, a workfare worker mentioned in Chapter 1 as an organizer of George's funeral, was about 5'5". She was heavily tattooed and weighed approximately two hundred pounds. She came to the soup kitchen community in March, 1984, soon after giving birth to

a baby who died a few hours after delivery. Barbara attributed the death to her husband, who, she said, punched her in the stomach. She had hitchhiked from Alabama in her ninth month of pregnancy and now was trying to reestablish herself in her home town of Middle City. She had lived in Hotel Paradise for many years. She often sat in the dining room, giving Sue support by listening to her stories, or by letting her stay in her room at the hotel when Sue had had a fight with her boyfriend. Sue told me how much Barbara had done for her—cooking for her, letting her stay in her room, and "getting her high." One day, before a talk on alcoholism began at the soup kitchen, Barbara said to the group "Wait. Let me get my friend [Sue] from downstairs. She needs to hear this!"

Barbara was one of the few guests who appeared comfortable at any table in the dining room and with any group, from the hotel men to the middle-aged women. She would sit at Peggy's table for a while, visit with the Gamache family, give Pedro a friendly hug, and joke and laugh with Alan.

Marcos

Probably the most outstanding example of a central figure in the soup kitchen was Marcos, a Puerto Rican man in his thirties, who spoke English well. Marcos had one badly crossed eye, and he told me that this had kept him out of many jobs he would have liked. In the years I knew him, he worked sporadically, installing washing machines. However, he had chronic pains in his lungs, which he told me his doctors had not diagnosed, but which had prevented him from doing heavy work.

Most often Marcos stood between the coffeepot and the entrance to the soup kitchen. From this visible spot he greeted people as they came down the stairs. He often interpreted the daily menu from English to Spanish in front of the one hundred guests. Marcos lived at the hotel, and his social network included the whites, blacks, and Puerto Ricans there as well as the Puerto Rican community within the soup kitchen. I saw Marcos interpret official forms for people, accompany them to the welfare office and to the hospital. He tried to provide them with character references when they needed to get into Windy Heights apartments. Well groomed, he was also rather unusual among the guests in that he occasionally owned a car. He viewed himself as a working person, although he spent most of his time out of work.

The Gamache Family: An Extended Family at the Soup Kitchen

On most mornings the Gamache sisters, Joan and Sally, and their children arrived at the soup kitchen together at ten o'clock, having walked about a mile from their apartments at a low-income housing project in the western part of town. Joan and Sally sat at a table close to the back entrance, near the old crib, broken high chairs, and the dirty rug. The mothers sat the five children at the table and brought them doughnuts and glasses of water, hoping they would sit quietly for two and a half hours, until lunch was served. This was a challenge, since most of the time the children became bored and restless. Much of the time they were yelled at or hit, apparently out of the mothers' frustrations at their interruptions. The children themselves seemed to feel comfortable in the soup kitchen setting. They helped themselves to the doughnuts and water, wandered up the stairs, and went around to other tables.

Sally and Joan were often joined by the rest of the Gamache family, which consisted of another sister, Nicole, age fifteen, and Marie, mother of the three young women. Marie's three daughters reflected the ethnicity of their fathers: Sally was white; Joan was darker than her mother and looked Latino; and Nicole, the darkest, was thought of as black by most of the soup kitchen community.

For most of the time I knew Nicole, she was out of school. She was tall, good-looking, and sat next to her sisters in the soup kitchen and smoked many cigarettes. During the spring of 1984, the Department of Juvenile Probation put pressure on Nicole to return to school. She refused to go, and was committed to the Department of Children and Youth Services, then placed in a group home in a neighboring community. During most of the school year, 1984–1985, she was not in the soup kitchen, though I saw her on the streets with her sisters on weekends.

Joan, the eldest, who was twenty-one, lived with her two children, Damon, age five, and Mary, two. Joan was tall, had long curly brown hair, an olive complexion, and was quite pretty except for her teeth, which were spaced far apart, and some of which were missing. She was the most outgoing of the family, and occasionally seemed to be the spokeswoman in approaching other people. She may also have been thought of as the most competent by the rest of her family. For example, in the spring of 1983, when I first was at the soup kitchen on a regular basis, it was Joan who asked me if I knew where Nicole, then fourteen, could get birth control pills. During this period, Joan was also "put in charge" of Sally, Jr., Sally's infant daughter, who was thought to have failure-to-thrive syndrome, and after several months, the infant did begin to gain weight.

Sally, twenty years old and weighing about two hundred pounds, was shorter than her sisters. She was not as communicative. She had a five-year-old son, Steve, who was committed by the Department of Children and Youth Services to the custody of his grandmother, Marie. In reality, Steve was often cared for at the soup kitchen by Sally herself. As a matter of fact, after June, 1984, when Marie went back to work, Sally "baby-sat" her own son during the daytime. She also had Maria, a four-year-old, and her baby, Sally, Jr. In the spring of 1985 Sally was due to give birth again. She told me that she had had enough children and planned to go to work as soon as this baby was born. She said that Joan would take care of all the children. As Sally related her plans to me, Joan was sitting at the table, absorbed in a comic book. Her lack of comment could be interpreted as acquiescence, resignation, suppressed anger, or some other feelings.

Joan and Sally most often sat smoking, talking to each other, and reading comic books. As more people came in, some joined them at their table. Most of their social network outside of their own family consisted of other young mothers with children, as well as some of the young men of the soup kitchen.

Much of the social network revolved around child-rearing. For example, one day as I sat talking to Joan and Sally, Linda, a young woman about 5'2" tall, weighing approximately 180 pounds, with several children of her own, saw Steve run up the church stairs. She said to him, "You little brat! I'm going to beat you!" Steve eventually came down the stairs without a beating. I watched Sally to see what her reaction was to Linda's threat, and she appeared to be unconcerned.

Throughout the years of sitting and talking to Joan and Sally, I observed that often their friends came over to yell at the children. There seemed to be some tacit agreement that it was all right for some of their friends to discipline the children. This example alerts us to the dangers of indiscriminately viewing all social support as improving the quality of life for everyone involved. The shared discipline of children might relieve the mothers, but it might also increase incidences of physical and verbal punishments of the children.

Often Alan sat with Joan and Sally. Although he was single and friendly toward them, he was not romantically involved with them. He often picked up the children if they were crying, and helped them to doughnuts. One day I observed Alan giving Joan the kind of social support that may be thought of as information and advice. She was telling us that she refused to send her Damon to kindergarten in the fall because "I don't want that school screwing up my kid like it did me." Alan looked surprised and said he thought it was the law to send children to kindergarten. Joan was adamant and said that she would keep Damon with her and "teach him at home." Alan again gently confronted her. Eventually, after the summer of 1984, Joan decided to send Damon to the kindergarten of the local Catholic school.

In the afternoons, Sally and Joan walked over to classes for the General Education Diploma (GED) that were held at the adult learning center, three blocks from the soup kitchen. Joan often took her school books with her to the soup kitchen, and she occasionally asked me to help her with homework. Sally appeared to have less interest in school, but she went along with the routine. One of the highlights of their year was the class's trip to Western City to shop for Christmas. It became their main topic of conversation for weeks ahead. Their enthusiasm seemed to point up the sparsity of their experiences outside of Middle City and the soup kitchen. Joan and Sally both said that the trip was very successful.

The Gamache family and the other members of their social network provided daily examples of support in the soup kitchen. There was almost daily tangible support given in the form of baby-sitting. There was informational support given, as when Joan told Nicole about birth control, and Alan gave Joan advice about sending her son to school. The emotional support was obvious in the constant communication at the Gamache table. Although this support could go on at other times within the family (though they did not actually live with each other), the support appeared to manifest itself most intensely in the soup kitchen setting.

The Support of the Soup Kitchen

In addition to the specific social support networks found at the soup kitchen, one might conceptualize the entire setting as a support system for the guests. In *Number Our Days*, Barbara Myerhoff (1978) demonstrates the supportiveness of a Jewish community center in Venice, California, for people in their eighties and nineties. As at the Tabernacle Soup Kitchen, there was always a changing group within the center, in this case due to death, hospitalizations, and moves to convalescent homes. The center remained a stable focal point in the lives of the elderly members and supplied a way to cope with loneliness and social isolation in a manner quite similar to the use of the soup kitchen for its guests.

One important difference was the high degree of member participation in the operation of the Jewish Community Center and in the planning of activities. This sense of participation, I believe, enhanced its supportiveness for its members. In the soup kitchen this sense of participation, and therefore of supportiveness, exists to a lesser extent.

Summary

Analysis of social networks is especially useful in viewing the world of guests at the soup kitchen. Although they may begin their association there as a way to mitigate feelings of loneliness and social isolation, or to find a place of acceptance for their deviant behavior, many, after a period of time in the soup kitchen, become part of a network of social relationships. The personal relationships that the individual builds up around him can then be seen to compensate for the lack of close-knit kin groups or formal membership in institutions such as the work force or other organizations.

There is mounting evidence that the existence of a social support network can lessen the negative consequences of life events, including physical illness, bereavement, unemployment, and alcoholism (Cobb 1976; Mitchell and Trickett 1980). The exact relationship between social support and the positive buffer effect is not always obvious, but the evidence points to the fact that tangible support, perceived emotional support, and informational support may all function differently in buffering the effects of illness and loss (Schaefer et al. 1981).

The Tabernacle Soup Kitchen provides an ideal setting in which to observe the (primarily) positive aspects of social networks and social support at work. I have described numerous instances of emotional, tangible, and informational support guests are able to provide for each other. As in any human group, some individuals are more able than others to give effective support. The next phase of the soup kitchen study was to discover if there was a way to enhance the supportive functions of these central figures within the social networks of the dining room.

9

Self-Help in the Dining Room:
Guests as Counselors

In order to explore the soup kitchen and more fully realize its potential for self-help, three pilot projects were conducted using the indigenous leadership of the guests. But before describing the soup kitchen self-help projects, let us review some of the experiences of indigenous help within other cultural contexts.

Throughout the world, there are examples of health care and other programs in which local people are trained to deliver services to their own group. This model is a way of bridging the cultural gap that often exists between the professional world and the world of the consumer of health or human services. At times, the indigenous worker is seen as the *only* way to reach underserved populations in a culturally congruent manner. Central to the idea of the indigenous worker is the identification of individuals within the group who are interested in learning new information and who have demonstrated leadership potential or who are central figures within their social network.

Perhaps the best-known example of the indigenous worker is the barefoot doctor of China (Rosenthal and Greiner 1982; You-Long and Li Min 1982; and Horn 1969). Barefoot doctors have brought essential health services to the 800 million people (80 percent of the population) living in China's rural areas (Sidel and Sidel 1973).

These indigenous workers undergo training that is less rigorous than the long-term education necessary for nursing and medical degrees, although during the 1980s there appears to have been a trend toward increased education for all health workers and a decreasing reliance upon the barefoot doctor (New and Cheung 1984). In addition to improved nutrition and public health measures, the work of the barefoot doctors is credited with contributing to increased life expectancy in China from twenty-eight years in 1935 (Yeh and Chow 1972) to over sixty-five years in 1983 (Sidel and Sidel 1982). In some Latin American countries, *promotores de salud* (health promoters) offer similar health services to both rural and urban medically underserved poor (Behrhorst 1975).

Within the United States, the most prominent example of the indigenous-worker strategy developed during the War on Poverty in the training of people referred to as "neighborhood workers." The neighborhood workers are people from the same ethnic, geographic, or income group as the community to be served. They are given on-the-job training and, ideally, ongoing professional supervision. The neighborhood worker movement began in 1964, with the creation of the Office of Economic Opportunity, and still exists today in a number of community action programs. One achievement of the indigenous workers was that people eligible for Aid to Families with Dependent Children (AFDC), but not receiving its benefits, were informed about the program by neighborhood workers. The result was a 107 percent increase in the AFDC caseload between 1960 and 1969, most of it occurring after the 1964 inception of the War on Poverty (Piven and Cloward 1971).

Examples of the barefoot doctors, *promotores de salud*, and neighborhood workers all involve the employment of the community members. The individuals usually enter a career system where they earn their own livelihood through this work. There are other instances, however, where the community member is recognized as a support person but is not in any way separated or removed from his status as a community member. Such was the case in a study of housekeepers in nursing homes. J. Neil Henderson (1981) demonstrated the extent of social and emotional support that was being provided by housekeepers in a convalescent home, in contrast with the lack of support provided by the nursing staff. In addressing groups of gerontologists and psychologists, Henderson pointed out that the discovery of these indigenous conveyors of support has the potential of promoting housekeeper/patient interaction and enhancing the respect (and possible monetary reward) of the housekeepers.

Another example of the indigenous worker concept is the mental health project described by Wiesenfeld and Weis (1979). They provided training to a group of ten hairdressers in supportive, nondirective counseling techniques. In previous research (1979), Cowen and associates had documented the extent and quality of the hairdresser/customer interactions relating to the social and emotional problems of the customers. This is an example of enhancing the strengths of already established and trusted members of an individual's (customer's) support network, without requiring a career change by the indigenous worker.

Self-Help in the Tabernacle Soup Kitchen

I became interested in testing the idea of self-help within the soup kitchen after I saw the general sociability and air of acceptance in that setting. I wanted to see if these attributes could be in any way enhanced through a training project for some of the guests. For example, if some of the guests affiliated with each other in social networks, could the amount of support within the network be increased? Could the advice people often give each other about resources in the community be based on more accurate information? Could the atmosphere of sociability and acceptance be enlarged to include some of the guests who are "loners"? Would a group of guests come to regularly scheduled classes, or would the continual life crises that I knew existed for most of the guests interfere? Would classes be perceived as too structured and alien to the nonthreatening ambiance of the soup kitchen?

In order to address some of these issues, I conducted three pilot projects in self-help within the soup kitchen in the spring of 1984, in the fall of 1985, and in the winter of 1987. The projects came to be known as the Tabernacle Soup Kitchen community counseling course. A total of twenty-one guests completed the course, with two guests taking it twice and one guest taking it three times. Each course consisted of approximately twelve hours of instruction, in twice-weekly sessions. Before each course began, I spent several weeks "on the scene" in order to search for guests whom others looked to for support and guidance, and I invited these guests to join the course. I also received suggestions from the soup kitchen director and from several guests who told me of their interest in the course and were invited to come. In addition, the director and I made several noontime announcements about the classes to the entire dining room in order to avoid excluding any guests who wanted to come.

Community Counseling Course of Spring, 1984
My first search for potential indigenous workers was in November, 1983, at which time the 74 guest respondents in a health survey were asked if they would be interested in attending a class in counseling and community resources in the soup kitchen. Of the 74, 42 (57 percent) said that they were interested. It was my impression that this high level of interest was due to the endemic boredom that plagued most of the guests. The emotion of boredom has been reported as a correlate of loneliness (Rubenstein and Shaver 1982) and seemed to be a dominant theme in the lives of the guests. In other words, they might have said "yes" to almost any proposal to "do something."

In May, 1984, several weeks before the classes were to begin, I looked for the 42 people on the initial list. By then, 15 (36 percent) were still guests of the soup kitchen on a regular basis. However, of the 15, one had become actively psychotic, one had returned to heavy drug use, and one person said that she was more interested in therapy than in learning to be a counselor. Of the remaining 12, four came to the first class. In addition to these four, the director suggested that we invite 14 people who had become regulars since

November and seemed to be focal people in social networks at the soup kitchen. Of this group, eight came to the first class.

Ideally the participants in the training course would be members of a social support network, and should have some of the traditionally defined leadership qualities, such as the "capacity to stimulate the group, mobilize activities, synthesize thinking" (Hartford 1971: 214), or be, in the words of the Inuit, "the one to whom all listen" (Nanda 1984: 274). However, not every guest who had some of these characteristics was interested in or able to participate in the training.

Peggy, for example, was a dominant person within a social network of soup kitchen regulars who were women in their thirties, forties, and fifties (see Chapter 8). She was the chief workfare employee and had a formal leadership position in the operation of the kitchen. She had the respect of many of the guests, who looked up to her as she gave out information about welfare programs (at times inaccurately) and passed judgment on the other guests by her comments and facial expressions. As often as she was approached by me and Christine, Peggy was not interested in the classes. She did, however, tell me that two people at her table were interested, and one became an active participant.

Doug was another regular who would have been an ideal member of the class. He spent almost every morning at the soup kitchen, and he often took in homeless young men to live with him. Doug was knowledgeable about available housing in the area, and showed me and some of the guests the bulletin board of apartment and room advertisements, telling us which landlords to stay away from. He also facilitated guests' getting work at the local ice cream shop where he sometimes was a maintenance worker. As the classes were about to begin, he was rehired in the laundry of a local hospital, so he felt he would not be available for the classes.

I had had experience in the training of indigenous workers in an antipoverty agency in the Puerto Rican community, and knew that frequent classes with experiential "hands-on" learning such as role-playing are most effective. The ten sessions were to include supportive counseling techniques (e.g., active listening and empathy), as well as a presentation of information on community resources in areas of interest to the participants. The areas of interest were to be decided on by the participants during the first class. A community professional in each of the areas was to be brought to the class (or a field trip was to be taken), so that the guest/worker would feel comfortable with at least one key individual within a human service agency, and would be more likely (perhaps) to recommend that service to the other guests.

Most of the classes were held in the large room above the dining room, except for three sessions during which the class visited community facilities or agencies. Baby-sitting was provided by a grant from a local foundation, in order to enable people with children to attend. The grant also paid for notebooks, pens, graduation certificates, and graduation presents of a cardboard file case for the numerous brochures and papers accumulated by the class participants. I gave the class bilingually, in English and in Spanish.

Six soup kitchen regulars, already described, successfully completed the course. They were Marie Gamache, who was the focal person of a social network that included her daughters, their children, and friends; Esther, the woman in her fifties who was disabled by arthritis; Alan, the low-skilled, sporadically employed young man, at times involved in a fundamentalist Protestant church; Pedro, the friendly middle-aged Puerto Rican man; Jane, the woman in her fifties who had the motor impairment that made her speech and gait awkward; and Barbara, the tattooed workfare kitchen worker who eventually became a spokesperson for the soup kitchen community as a whole.

There was also Sue, the recovering victim of coma. Sue referred to herself as a "visitor" rather than a class participant. She told me that she could not visualize herself as being of any help to anyone else since she could barely keep track of her own life. Sue was, in fact, a very lively class participant when she did attend, and I felt that she could be of help to some of the other young women who lived at the Hotel Paradise as she did.

In addition to these people, six guests began the classes but did not complete the training sessions. It is instructive to compare the two groups. The six who completed the classes included two men and four women, whereas the six who did not complete the session included five men and one woman. The group who completed the course included two guests in their twenties, three in their forties, and one in his fifties. The group who did not complete the course included one guest in his teens, two in their twenties, and three in their thirties. The guests who were able to sustain interest in the course, therefore, included more women and were somewhat older than those who did not complete the training. It was also significant that only two of the guests who were actively engaged in the care of young children attended any of the classes. Perhaps in designing future indigenous worker programs in soup kitchens that have a population of children and parents, it would be desirable to discover how one might involve more of the young parents.

During the first class, the participants were asked to name the problems they thought were most relevant to themselves and the other guests of the soup kitchen. Their list included problems relating to finances, drugs and alcohol, housing, employment, handicaps, youth, family, and mental health. All of these topics were subsequently covered in the course. Absent from the list were child abuse and neglect, issues that had affected most, if not all, of the class. As I came to know the guests of the class, I realized that almost all of them had been affected by child abuse, both as victims and, among some who had had children, as abusers. My hypothesis is that this is a subject too close to home and too fraught with emotion to be suggested as a topic. I thought that, given the relevance of the issue of child-rearing to the soup kitchen population, subsequent training projects should find some way of incorporating the topic in an acceptable manner.

Professionals in the community were invited to present materials to the class on each topic. Most of the professionals were enthusiastic about the indigenous worker concept, and they treated the participants in the class with respect. One counselor, when she saw the group, asked me, "What kind of class is this again?" as if to say this did not look like a traditional class. One of the employment counselors canceled her session one hour before the class was to begin, saying she was "working on a grant." I wondered if she would have had the same disregard for a group she perceived to be more prestigious.

The participants appeared to be able to absorb much of the information provided by the community professionals. The social worker at an antipoverty agency discussed legal rights in applying for town welfare, an issue faced by many of the soup kitchen guests because town assistance workers have been known to harass potential recipients in order to discourage them from applying for welfare. The housing expert discussed the increasing shortage of low-income apartments. Out of the discussion (as well as other efforts) came a program that has gathered funds to be used to pay security deposits for people on town welfare who would otherwise not be able to move out of their rooms at the single-room-occupancy hotel and boarding houses. Barbara became the soup kitchen community representative to the group of professionals involved with this housing effort.

Another highlight of the classes was the talk given by a drug and alcohol counselor who was a former heroin addict. Before the class session began, Barbara invited Sue, a heavy drug and alcohol user, to the class. The participants all had had experience, or were close to someone who had had experience in drug and alcohol use. They were particularly interested in drug combinations and their cumulative effect. The class was also invited to tour the local therapeutic community, which none of the class members had ever entered.

During one of the sessions, a community nutritionist brought snacks for the group, which were examples of nutritious, economical foods. She also brought empty boxes of common products to demonstrate the art of reading the ingredients list. In addition she brought a seven-foot mannequin, with detachable internal organs, with which she demonstrated digestive processes. The class was lively and the participants were open-minded about trying the somewhat unorthodox foods suggested by the nutritionist.

The most confrontational class took place at the local mental health clinic. We met at the clinic with four members of the treatment staff to learn about the treatment modalities offered. As the session began, Jane broke into a tirade of tears and anger, stating how little the clinic had helped her when she was caring for her dying mother, who was engaging in bizarre behavior. The director of services said that the clinic does not usually make home visits, except to the Hispanics, who feel that they are essential. This reply made Jane even angrier. Sue (who had been coming to most of the classes since her visit to the drug and alcohol session) talked about her dislike of the clinic's psychiatric halfway house, and how she had purposely broken all of the rules so she would be thrown out. At the end of the session, Marie, who had been uncharacteristically quiet for the full session, stated that the clinic had done nothing for her and her fourteen-year-old daughter, Nicole, who was truant from school, and whom the courts were threatening to send to a reform school. To this, the clinic spokesperson said that the clinic was better able to handle mental health problems than social problems (a rather false dichotomy, I thought). At the end of the class, we all waited for Marie as she left the group and went to confront the counselor in charge of her daughter's case.

It was during this session that the potential power of a group of service consumers became evident. The guests, usually treated as passive clients of the mental health clinic, became vocal advocates for themselves in their roles as participants in a group setting. It is difficult to assess the impact of Marie's confrontation, but her daughter was eventually sent to a group home which is often considered (by mental health professionals) a better alternative to remaining on the streets or going to reform school.

Toward the end, the minister of Saint Mary's sat with the class. He entered a session of role-playing in various problem situations with the class. Each class member took a turn in helping him with his "problem." This session, which occurred spontaneously, functioned as an informal test of the knowledge acquired from the class. It also impressed the minister with the project's effectiveness.

At the completion of the training course, a graduation ceremony was held during the noon hour at the soup kitchen, in front of a hundred or so guests. The minister, in saying a prayer before the meal, said, "We thank you, God, for permitting some of us to learn how to be helpful to our soup kitchen community." A list of the names of the six guests who completed the training was then posted in a prominent place near the coffeepot, and Christine continued to make public reference to the graduates of the program for several weeks. Thus, for at least several weeks, many of the soup kitchen guests knew that there was a group of guests who were knowledgeable about community resources and could potentially be of help.

Evaluation and Analysis: Spring, 1984

The evaluation of a social program is extremely difficult because of the numerous confounding variables involved in addressing any complex social issue, and because of the often global nature of most program goals. Many fully funded social programs have to rely on "contextual" or "process" evaluations (Britan 1978; Bogdan and Biklen 1982), which essentially describe a program but do not measure its outcome in behavioral terms. The indigenous worker project of the Tabernacle Soup Kitchen was especially difficult to evaluate, in large part because the helping process that might have taken place was within the sphere of private conversations.

One of the hypothesized outcomes of the training program was that the participants might begin to feel a greater sense of confidence in themselves by completing twenty hours of training, meeting professionals on more equal ground than usually occurred for them, and in being viewed as people competent to give others information. In an attempt to measure this objectively, a short survey of open-ended questions was administered to each of the participants during the first and last sessions. However, although three of the posttests indicated an improved outlook on life when compared with the pretests, the guests did not write enough in their answers to provide any clear "evaluation." Although all the guests were literate in reading and writing (one in Spanish and the rest in English), they were not fluent enough to write answers to open-ended questions.

In order to assess the impact the indigenous workers might have had on the other soup kitchen guests, two follow-up sessions were held. During the first session, two weeks after the end of the program, Alan, Marie, Barbara, and Esther said that they had been approached by guests who wanted to know more about employment and housing programs. During this session, we also discussed the situation of Madeline, a guest who was acting in a rather bizarre manner in the dining room, walking about aimlessly, carrying an old rock magazine wherever she went, and spending inexplicably long periods of time in the ladies' room. The response from the group was that they wanted to stay far away from this guest, so that she would not "hit" them.

This example pointed up a major complication. If one of the class members did become involved with this disturbed guest, it would be impossible to end the relationship at one o'clock in the afternoon, when the soup kitchen ended. The class participants were all members of the low-income communities and would not be able to turn off their contacts at five o'clock the way middle-class professionals do. In other words, it appeared that they were making rational, self-protective, decisions about those guests with whom they would and would not become involved.

The second follow-up session occurred in the fall, three months after the completion of the course. When I asked the group if other guests had approached them for advice, Barbara and Alan said that guests they knew continued to ask them for suggestions. Jane and Esther reported, in rather disappointed tones, that they were not asked. Pedro said very little during this session, and Marie was unable to attend because she was by then working full-time.

The most dramatic outcome of the project occurred with Marie and Barbara. Immediately after the training ended, Marie entered a job-training program, and remained employed at an egg factory. Barbara continued to work at the soup kitchen for six months after the course. During that time she moved out of the hotel and into an apartment. While still on workfare, she joined a training course for kitchen workers held at the soup kitchen and graduated from it. She was then hired at a local fast-food restaurant and was still working there over a year later. She was being trained for a management position. She also spoke in public on the needs of the guests of the soup kitchen, and was a regular member of the committee of professionals that was funding the security deposits for apartments of recipients of town welfare. Both Marie and Barbara were fully employed, off of welfare programs, and no longer soup kitchen regulars, although Marie occasionally visited on her days off. Whether or not these changes would have occurred without the classes is impossible to know, but we can hypothesize that they were at least in part due to the influence of the project.

Alan continued to work at various jobs and began to talk about applying to college. He became a leader of a local tenants' rights organization and was involved in helping conduct a local politician's campaign. He later brought a teenager to a youth service agency, telling the counselor there that he had learned of the agency from the community counseling classes of two years before.

The project appeared to have the least effect on Esther, Pedro, and Jane, whose lives seemed to remain much as they were at the beginning of the program. However, Christine mentioned to me often in the years following the program how much more confident all six of the class members seemed to be.

The two "successes" point to an important difference between the indigenous worker in more traditional cultures in which the idea has been tried, and the indigenous worker idea in the soup kitchen. In other cultures, successful workers are expected to remain within the culture, at least for a period of time. On the other hand, "success" in terms of the soup kitchen culture often means finding employment and then leaving the soup kitchen.

Community Counseling Course: Fall, 1985

In an attempt to evaluate the idea of the indigenous worker training project in the soup kitchen, it seemed important to try to replicate the classes. If the idea is a valuable one, then it should be repeatable with another group of guests. To this end, I presented the community counseling classes again in the fall of 1985. The director, Christine, was also interested in seeing another group of guests gain information from training, since she had been very positive about the outcome of the first classes.

In preparing the second series, I had an opportunity to refine aspects of the course. I still hoped to attract the central figures of various social networks, but this time I was more convinced that *any* guest who came to the dining room on a regular basis was in fact part of the soup kitchen culture. This was true whether they regularly sat within a network of other guests or whether they sat alone and with a different group of strangers every day. I was less concerned with whether the sharing of information on community resources occurred within or outside the dining room. In other words, although we might speak of a soup kitchen culture, and although the classes were intended for the guests inside the dining room, the "inside" versus "outside" distinction seemed artificial in relation to the dissemination of information. I had come to feel that the sharing of useful information with any members of the low-income, unemployed community would be useful.

I was also interested in reaching the group of young parents who were a significant group within the dining room, but whom the first classes had not reached. During the second series of classes, I was able to attract a central figure in the young parents' network, and one of the class sessions was devoted to issues of young parents, including child abuse and neglect. This time, I suggested the speaker, and she introduced issues that this group was willing to discuss.

In practical terms, I felt that the two-hour classes of the first course had been too long, and the new format incorporated one-hour classes twice a week. In this way I retained the consistency of twice-weekly classes, but the time frame for each class was more congruent with the group, whose attention span tended to be closer to one hour than to two.

I also abandoned the idea of evaluation through written pretest and posttest. I felt that this was an artificial method of testing the self-help concept. I also realized that follow-up information would take as long as one to two years to collect, after the classes had ended. In other words, by the end of the fall of 1985, there would be very tentative follow-up information.

I began the second series of classes in the fall of 1985. Christine introduced me to several guests whom she identified as indigenous leaders. In addition, I spent several weeks introducing myself to guests I did not know. Since approximately two-thirds of the soup kitchen population had changed since the classes had last been offered, there were many guests to approach as potential participants.

The project began with fourteen people expressing interest, ten of whom attended one of the first two classes. Seven graduated from the course by coming to more than half of the fourteen sessions.

The topics were similar to those in the first sessions, with the addition of talks by the doctor from the health clinic, a social worker from the Puerto Rican agency, and a counselor for teenage parents.

The guests who completed the course were again men and women whose main common feature was the substantial amount of time they spent in the soup kitchen. They all were somewhat bored with their life-style, which is probably what attracted them to the class.

Marcos, a soup kitchen leader, described in Chapter 8, was an excellent class member. He attended regularly and was able to think of friends who needed help from the agencies we learned about. For example, when the group met at the mental health clinic, the victim-assistance counselor talked about services for victims of crimes, and Marcos thought of many people he could recommend to the counselor.

Joan, the oldest daughter of the Gamache family, was an active class member. She talked to the alcohol counselor about a group of young people she knew who were all involved with alcohol and heroin. The counselor made plans with Joan to meet with this group. Joan also followed up on a job program talked about by one of the speakers, and asked me to accompany her.

Esther was a graduate of the class of the spring of 1984, but decided to join this class again. I felt that she was almost a coteacher, since she often compared the speakers of the two classes. I was impressed with how much she remembered from the previous sessions. For example, she remembered all the foods the first nutritionist had presented to the group, especially the violet petals and the popcorn sprinkled with brewer's yeast.

Beth was an enthusiastic class member who was usually the first of the group to arrive at the soup kitchen. I often found her sitting at a table, reading over her notes from the previous class. She appeared to use the classes to discuss her own personal problems, talking about her drinking with the alcohol counselor, her abused childhood with the teenage parents' counselor, and her mental health problems when we went to the mental health clinic. Beth was one of the most isolated of the guests, and she seemed to use the class as a vehicle for having some social interaction. I saw her become more and more comfortable in the group as the weeks progressed, in that she would initiate conversations with other class members.

Arnold was a single man in his late forties who described himself as a recovering alcoholic. He had spent many years living in the Hotel Paradise, although he had recently moved out of it. He, like Joan, Marcos, and Esther, was a part of a friendship group that met at the soup kitchen. Like Marcos, he often thought of friends who could use the service of an agency we were hearing about. Toward the latter part of the course, Arnold had surgery on his elbow, and although he only missed three classes, the surgery seemed to interrupt his concentration. He appeared interested, and with encouragement could be an influential leader in the soup kitchen.

The two most marginal members of the class were Ismael and Pat. As the course progressed, it became clear that Ismael was getting into more and more trouble. He was arrested toward the end of the course for stealing credit cards, having drug paraphernalia, and possessing marijuana. I thought that he was probably addicted to a variety of drugs. Nevertheless, he came to almost all of the classes and was able to participate, usually relating his own problems to each speaker. On the day of graduation, Ismael was in the drug and alcohol unit of a psychiatric hospital.

Pat, the woman in her forties whose daughter had died of cystic fibrosis, had returned to the soup kitchen in order to help in the kitchen. She volunteered for the classes and appeared enthusiastic about them. However, I noticed that I had to tell her several times that the class was beginning, and she seemed hesitant to leave the company of the women who were volunteers in the kitchen. I think that she may have seen going to the classes with the guests as a step down in status from that of a kitchen volunteer. Although she had been a guest, and was still a friend and a neighbor of many of the people in the dining room, she spent most of her time in the kitchen. In contrast to the others who were eager for the sessions, she seemed resistant to them.

The classes again ended with a graduation ceremony in the dining room, at which all of the participants (except Ismael), their friends, other soup kitchen guests, and the community professionals were present. A certificate was handed to each graduate, and a list of their names was posted in the dining room near the coffeepot for all to see.

Evaluation and Analysis: Fall, 1985

As discussed earlier, all the effects of a project of this type were not immediately apparent. All the participants were still soup kitchen regulars. Marcos began working as a security guard at a local institution on the second shift soon after the end of the course. He was able to keep the job for a full year. He began living with Sandy, another guest, who had two children from a previous marriage. He and Sandy came to the soup kitchen each morning together. Joan signed up for job training through a federal project, but had not yet, in fact, begun training. Esther told me that she felt that she was at a standstill in life, and asked me for some information regarding college. Beth continued to come to the soup kitchen every day, though she still sat alone. Pat was still a kitchen volunteer. Ismael was in prison serving time for his drug activities.

Community Counseling Course: Winter, 1987

A third community counseling course began in the winter of 1987. At least some of the recruiting was now accomplished by the guests who had been involved with the previous courses. Three of the graduates of the first courses—Esther, Arnold, and Marcos—decided to join the course again. The classes lasted for six weeks and met for one hour twice a week. Topics included welfare, alcohol and drug rehabilitation services, health, mental health, employment, education, rape crisis, and battered women's services. In addition the supervisor of the local protective service agency came to discuss child abuse and neglect. Most of the members of the class had had direct contact with protective services, having been reported (or "turned in," in soup kitchen vernacular) for suspected abuse or neglect of their children. Despite the potential for embarrassment and mistrust, the supervisor and the guests appeared to like and trust each other.

In this series of classes all eight guests who started the course completed it. The course also included two community workers who wanted to join in order to improve their own knowledge of community resources. At the end of twelve sessions, a graduation ceremony was held in the dining room to present the graduates to the soup kitchen community.

Among the graduates, Marcos, Esther, and Arnold have been described earlier.

I had known Debbie as a guest for two years. In her midforties, she was a capable woman who had been to college for two years. She had married and divorced a man in the armed services, and they had an adopted son, Tom, who was also a soup kitchen regular. Debbie, who told me that her problem in life was alcoholism, was a member of Alcoholics Anonymous. In addition to our course, she was in training to help a community health worker take blood pressure.

Sandy was in her late thirties. She lived with Marcos and her two children from a previous marriage. Sandy told me that she had been constantly beaten by her husband, and much of the time she appeared to be in pain from head and backaches. She was a very articulate class member. During one session she presented information she had collected on a weatherization program offered by a local utility company.

I had met José, a Puerto Rican man in his late thirties, one morning in the winter of 1985 when, in an inebriated state, he asked me to help him stop drinking. After spending several hours with me visiting a local alcohol rehabilitation program, he had gone back to his room to sleep. However, some time during the following year, he got some control over his drinking, and he had been a workfare worker in the soup kitchen for approximately one year before the course began. José was a tall, good-looking man who was fluent in Spanish and English.

Violet was Peggy's daughter, who had recently moved to Middle City from another part of the state in order to run away from an abusive husband. She lived with her two children, and often told the class that she received visits from the protective service worker, whom she referred to as "Uncle John." Violet was a good-looking young woman and appeared to spend time dressing up for the class. She took voluminous notes and perhaps more than any other guest seemed to be oriented to the role of student.

Alice was a regular at Peggy's table and was in the soup kitchen almost every day that I was, from the spring of 1983 through the spring of 1987. She lived with her husband and three children in Middle City. She often complained that her husband drank and that he "wouldn't let her" do things such as cut her hair or get a baby-sitter for the children. On most mornings Alice wore a neckbrace and looked drowsy. She asked Sandy or Violet to take notes for her, since she could not read or write.

Evaluation of Winter, 1987, Course

The third course appeared to have gone the best. The attendance was good (almost all of the guests came every time), and there was a great deal of communication among the guests.

One person whose situation did change was Arnold. Soon after the completion of the course, his ten-year-old daughter and a boy of eight came to visit him for a week. Then Arnold's former wife, who had custody of the daughter, and the boy (not related to either Arnold or his wife), said that she had nowhere to live and that Arnold would have to rear the two children. He became busy, involved with the schools, protective services, and other guests in his attempt to make a home for the children.

Since the course, José has been hired by Saint Mary's Church to be the sexton, which means that he is no longer on welfare. Debbie

continues to take blood pressures, and has been involved in an effort
of community leaders to buy land on which to develop affordable
housing for low and moderate income people.

The Potential for AIDS Prevention in the Soup Kitchen

The soup kitchen is an ideal setting for implementing self-help
philosophy regarding prevention and early detection of Acquired
Immune Deficiency Syndrome (AIDS). The dining room of the soup
kitchen is a daily meeting place of many of Middle City's intravenous
drug users. They congregate around the coffeepot to talk and drink
coffee. A self-help program, using the indigenous leaders of the
drug-using network within the dining room, would be a logical
extension of the community counseling courses. An AIDS self-help
course could concentrate on recruiting guests from the drug-user
group and their friends, and focus on information regarding the
prevention of AIDS through drug rehabilitation, the use of sterile
needles for the untreated drug user, and the promotion of sexual
practices that are considered safe.

The Self-Help Philosophy in Soup Kitchens

In many ways, a soup kitchen is an ideal setting in which to
implement social change through the self-help philosophy. Individuals come to the soup kitchen on a regular basis and create an
identifiable culture that fosters a sociable, accepting atmosphere.
Inevitably, some of the members of the culture become leaders, and
some become central figures within social networks.

The ideal of attracting these leaders and central figures to a self-
help project is more difficult to realize than one might anticipate.
As we have seen, some of the leaders have no interest in coming to
a structured situation such as classes. On the other hand, some of
the most interested class members are the loners, who perhaps see
the classes as a way of joining a social network. Further, the theory

that soup kitchen guests could be encouraged to reach out beyond their own network boundaries to other guests was perhaps unrealistic, given the difficulty some might encounter in developing a relationship with someone from whom one could not easily escape in daily life. Finally, those individuals who appear to be most able to absorb new information may use the information for themselves and then leave the soup kitchen culture by joining the work force.

Despite these limitations, the self-help idea that was implemented through the community counseling classes achieved some measure of success. The classes themselves were seen as a positive activity by the guests and staff of the soup kitchen. Class participants appeared to gain some increased self-esteem as members of the project. They were able to sustain interest in the classes over a five- or six-week period, and appeared able to absorb the information presented to them about community resources. The classes themselves seemed to provide a pleasant respite from the boredom of their current life.

Classes within a soup kitchen are a good way to test aspects of the self-help philosophy. The concept of classes does not imply that anyone has a "problem" that needs "treatment." Rather, classes embody the spirit of self-help by beginning with the assumption that guests have the ability to learn important information and then to share it with other people. The soup kitchen is an ideal setting in which to expand further the ideas of self-help with some of the individuals whose lives fall outside of the affluence of the rest of North American society.

10

Staff Philosophy and the Concept of Ministry

As the preceding chapters have demonstrated, the Tabernacle Soup Kitchen creates an atmosphere wherein the guests' desires for sociability, for acceptance, and for some degree of human alliance are satisfied. Does this atmosphere, so rare for the underclass who are excluded from work places and from stable family relationships, come about spontaneously in the dining room of 100 guests, or is it created by the soup kitchen staff?

What kinds of skills and resources must a staff person have who is providing a safe harbor for soup kitchen guests? What kind of personal and professional philosophy is necessary to work with people who are often disheveled in appearance, may be intoxicated on drugs or alcohol, may be hallucinating, and appear to have few plans beyond eating the noontime meal at the soup kitchen? How is it possible for the staff to work in a setting without the traditional symbols of social control, in which the roles and power of the client and staff are clear?

Ministry and the Soup Kitchen

One of the possible answers to the question of how soup kitchen staff persons cope with their jobs is that he/she is often religious.

138

They appear to see at least a part of their mission in life as service to the poor.

The concept of ministry is one that appears to grow from an interpretation of Christianity (Rendle 1984). In an excellent discussion of the concept of ministry, the Reverend Gilbert R. Rendle, Jr., describes the serving of strangers as being an opportunity to confront God, who may be personified by a "stranger."

> It has been a stroke of God's grace to experience how nervous, self-conscious middle class people whose identity, happiness and self worth are tied to job, possessions and community status can be moved by people who continue to be happy and have feelings of worth—yet have no job, possessions or status. . . . For ministry is possible when we are able to convert our hostilities (our racism, classism, sexism, ageism) to hospitality which will allow us to convert our enemies (those most unlike us) into our guests (those valued for their differences). Ministry discovers that in seeking to help others who become our guests, we paradoxically experience God's grace in our own lives. (Rendle 1984: 467)

The Catholic Worker Movement also has long addressed the meaning of work with the poor in sheltering environments. The Movement espouses pacifism, personalism (individual action to achieve social justice), and living in the community in voluntary poverty (Roberts 1984). Their Houses of Hospitality, initiated by the founder of the Movement, Dorothy Day, offer food and shelter to the poor. The staff, most of whom are volunteers, lives in the shelters with the guests. One of the editors of the Movement's newspaper, the *Catholic Worker*, was Michael Harrington, author of *The Other America* (1961), the book that has often been credited with raising the consciousness of poverty in the United States, and of helping to initiate the War on Poverty.

A recent issue of the newsletter *The Catholic Agitator* discusses some of the underpinnings of the philosophy of the Hospitality Soup Kitchen of Los Angeles:

A simple meal has always been at the very heart of the Catholic Worker tradition. For me the meal we serve at our soup kitchen is a daily miracle which brings with it the gift of hope. It nourishes the poor and hungry and at the same time feeds the souls of those who despair that the world will never change, that brother will forever take up arms against brother, that the poor will always be oppressed, and that self-interest will continue to act as the primary motivating force in human affairs.

We have produced something of a minor miracle, a daily transformation of discards into a delicious meal—a feast for 1,000 hungry people—costing a total of only $5.00. . . . It is a small act of hope that fills an emptiness deeper than mere physical hunger. . . .

It is a simple meal that feeds the poor and continues to give hope during this Easter season. It is the bread of Eucharist, the Matzoh of Passover, the communion meal that inspires in us a wild, improbable hope that all human beings may one day sit down at the same table as brothers and sisters, members of a single human family, and break bread together. (Dietrich 1985: 3)

I am suggesting that soup kitchen staffs view their jobs as opportunities to act on their religious faith, so that the usual professional concerns of improvement and meeting treatment goals becomes less relevant. On the other hand, soup kitchen staffs often comprise members of the professional middle-class community who may feel the effects of their professional training in the soup kitchen, despite their religious commitment. This dual commitment may result in periods of ambivalence for the soup kitchen staffperson. It is a fruitful area for future research in which to discover the range and quality of personal philosophies and coping styles within soup kitchen staffs.

Many of the guests themselves are conscious that the soup kitchen is related to a church. For example, when I meet the Puerto Rican guests on the streets of Middle City, they often say, "Te veo en la iglesia" (I'll see you in the church). Finally, the community in general indicates its view of the soup kitchen in religious terms, as at

Thanksgiving and Christmastime, when the soup kitchen is inundated with donations of food. The area churches and organizations appear to use these periods of religious fervor as a time to act on their feelings through donations to the soup kitchen.

Although this study did not survey all of the soup kitchens in the state, the four others I visited were directed by people closely affiliated with Christian churches. The community soup kitchen in a town in the most rural area of the state was secularly administered by a community organization but was staffed by a deacon of the Catholic church. Another secularly administered soup kitchen in a large city was staffed by a woman who later joined a convent. The remaining two soup kitchens were directed by nuns and were administered through a mission of the Catholic church. Within the Tabernacle Soup Kitchen, in addition to the two directors, the nurse was a religious Catholic, and the assistant director was the wife of a local Protestant minister.

Directors of the Tabernacle Soup Kitchen

A description of some of the work of the people who have directed the Tabernacle Soup Kitchen offers us some insight into how staff may cope with running a soup kitchen on a day-to-day basis. The first director of the Tabernacle Soup Kitchen was Jean (see Chapter 3), a widow in her middle twenties, with a young child. Jean was a highly energetic person who spent much of her time speaking to local organizations in efforts to obtain money, food, and volunteer workers for the soup kitchen. She told me that she became involved in the soup kitchen after she met the Reverend Smith, the minister who initiated the Tabernacle Soup Kitchen, when she was a welfare worker. She told me that she had been looking for something more in her life. Jean converted to Christianity, joined Saint Mary's Church, and became the director of the soup kitchen. She told me that her biggest problem during her two years there was the lack of support she felt from the administration of Saint Mary's. Soon after the founding of the soup kitchen, the Reverend Smith left the parish.

His replacements (there had been four new ministers and assistant ministers by 1987), Jean felt, never had the dynamism and commitment of the Reverend Smith. Furthermore, he was able to serve as a buffer between Jean and some of the parishioners who felt that the soup kitchen was an unsightly presence in their midst. After two years Jean left, disappointed, went on to graduate school in one of the human services. She has severed her ties to Christianity. Jean's directorship of the soup kitchen could be seen as a part of her relationship to Christianity. She told me that her greatest satisfaction had been her relationship with the guests and the community volunteers.

After Jean left, Christine became the director of the Tabernacle Soup Kitchen (see Chapter 3). Christine often spoke directly of her commitment to Christianity. She wore a cross around her neck, and it was she who instituted a daily prayer before the meal in the soup kitchen. She appeared to be a more structured person than Jean, and her personal life seemed to offer a greater degree of comfort and stability. During her first several months, Christine made a series of changes which gave the soup kitchen a less chaotic, more organized atmosphere. She moved her office from the floor above the dining room to the area in back of the dining room and kitchen, which put her in better touch with the guests and the workers.

Christine supervised the workfare kitchen crew consistently. If someone came in sick or high on drugs, she sent them home. One day, she told one of the women who smelled strongly of feces, that she needed to take a bath before she handled the food. Christine began procedures that improved the cleanliness and sanitation of food preparation. She also did away with the long line that formed every day for the meal. This line was a great source of tension, as people vied for the first spot. Meals had been served through a little window that separated the kitchen from the dining room. Christine had everyone seated *before* the meal, and called up each table, one at a time (varying the order each day). The guests now passed a serving table in the dining room and were served by volunteers and workfare workers who prepared the meal. In this way the meal was served in a more personalized manner.

Christine also began paying more attention to the nutritional content of the meals. Whereas Jean had left the decisions of food preparation up to the volunteers and workfare workers (a favorite was pancakes and sausage), Christine made the food decisions. She worked with several community nutritionists, to include enough meat, milk, vegetable, fruit, and bread each day. Christine also decided to remove doughnuts from the dining room by 11:30, so that guests (especially the children) still had an appetite for the meal itself. Finally, she concentrated her energies on activities inside the soup kitchen. For example, during the first six months of her directorship she declined invitations to participate in many community activities, concentrating on making the soup kitchen operate in a more organized and less frantic manner.

Jean and Christine both greeted every guest every day, and knew almost all of the guests by name. Because many of the guests utilize the soup kitchen over a period of time, the director has an opportunity to observe and remark on how a person is doing. For example, one day Christine said to John, a young man on workfare, "You seem to be getting thinner and thinner—are you eating these days?" To this John admitted that he had not been taking good care of himself. One day when Marilyn asked Christine for a safety pin for her pants, Christine was able to deduce that Marilyn too was losing weight due to some life crisis.

The conflict between professional goals of improvement and the religious orientation of nurturing was expressed by Rachel, the nurse who worked half-time for the Tabernacle Soup Kitchen for six months. She told me that despite her training in public health with Native American and rural people in South America, she found the lack of goals of the guests, as well as of herself, difficult. Many of the guests appeared to have little, or only fleeting, interest in their own health because they were struggling to materially survive the day. She finally found a useful role for herself by giving informal health education, seated at a different table each day with the guests. She was also an active health advocate for guests within the health system. She organized blood pressure screenings and dental hygiene instruction for the children. However, Rachel left the soup kitchen after six months and recommended to the City Ministry committee that they not hire another nurse, since the job was too frustrating.

Social Control in the Soup Kitchen

One of the inherent, though generally unacknowledged, characteristics of contemporary health and human service agencies is the social control the agency and staff have over their clients. Social control may be in the form of requiring some special behavior of clients in order that they receive a service, or maybe a requirement of special behavior once they are inside the service system. For example, the town welfare agency in Middle City requires that most of its recipients work for fifteen to twenty hours a week (workfare). In exchange, the individual receives a grant and an extra $10 a week "incentive pay." Social control may be the abstention from drug and alcohol use that is required of all residents of a drug and alcohol halfway house.

Social control is also exerted by the social distance that professionals often put between themselves and their clients. In human services, social distance often takes the form of referring to clients with words such as *manipulative* and *unmotivated*. Once this distance is achieved, control becomes easier since clients are not involved in the decision-making that goes on about them. These decisions often have enormous consequences for the individual, such as whether or not children are removed from a family, or whether a person is committed to a mental hospital. The medical professionals perhaps have been the best-known users of social distance, with their uniforms, their use of the pronoun *we*, and their scientific-sounding language. In total institutions, social control is exerted through the use of keys to locked areas, and the kinds of dress inmates (to use the term of Erving Goffman 1961) and staff wear. The physical layout of an institution can also exert control. For example, in many institutions the dormitories and dayrooms are arranged so that a few staff members can supervise many inmates or patients at one time (Goffman 1961).

Another common way to implement social control in the modern agency is through the labeling process that is widely used in various human service fields, especially mental health. This labeling can be viewed as the "medicalization of deviance" (Conrad and Schneider 1980) in that it views behavior that deviates from the norm (especially in socially unacceptable ways) as a condition of illness. The individual may receive an all-encompassing label, such as psychosis, which then has tremendous social consequences for him, or the label may be more fleeting, such as calling a person "hostile" when he is angry at a landlord who won't rent an apartment to him. These terms sound humanitarian but, in fact, serve to distance the staff and the client or patient, and ensure that the power and control remain in staff hands.

In contrast, the soup kitchen utilizes few of these mechanisms of social control. Despite the fact that there is a high ratio of guests to staff (approximately 50 to 1) there are no uniforms, no diagnoses, and no records of any kind kept about the guests. Most of the day, the staff (director and assistant director) are in the dining room with 80 to 100 people, or are in the kitchen with the volunteers and the workfare crew. Although the director does have an office, it is also used for food storage and so has an informal aura. There is no separate bathroom for staff people; this also symbolizes the diminished barriers between guests and staff.

The social control in the soup kitchen is subtle and appears to come about because of the relationship the director has with each guest. In this way she can confront behavior that is threatening the group.

For example, one morning two young men who were new to the soup kitchen were helping take down chairs from the tables. Interspersed in their loud conversation was "fuck this, fuck that." Christine appeared and asked them to please not use that language since they were in a church. The tone of the men's conversation immediately changed. On another occasion, I saw Christine ask a man, who was visibly intoxicated and was still drinking out of a bottle covered

by a paper bag, to please stop drinking or to leave. He left, got rid
of the bottle, and returned.

Christine also told me that she relied on the guests themselves to
help her control potentially dangerous or volatile behavior. One day
as I was sitting at a table with several women who came to the soup
kitchen daily, we all saw a heavy-set man come in, take out a big
roll of money, and appear to give the money to some of the guests
who came up to talk to him. The women told me that he shouldn't
be allowed in the soup kitchen—that he was a big drug dealer who
was paying off some of his contacts. I suggested that they tell Christine what was going on, but they wanted me to tell her. Later in the
morning I did, and she talked with a soup kitchen regular who was
involved with the dealer, saying that he (the regular) was welcome
to the kitchen, but to please have him leave his "bad business"
outside. Christine told me that the guest understood, is still a regular, and did not seem to tie Christine's confrontation to the women
or to me.

Peer Support and Soup Kitchen Staff

The soup kitchen is a setting without the sources of peer camaraderie of the traditional agency. Does the staff compensate for their
absence? To a limited extent they do—seeking out alternatives to
peer support—in their attendance at conferences on issues such as
hunger and poverty and in the occasional case review or community
effort in which they may be involved. For example, the director has
been a key person in an effort to provide a community fund for
security deposits on apartments for people on assistance programs
that do not grant security deposits. Another example is the director's
inclusion in case conferences concerning an abused child. When the
soup kitchen staff is brought to a case conference, they become part
of a "treatment team" and are included in a peer support system,
however briefly.

Staff Burnout

In recent years a great deal of literature has been devoted to the issue of burnout—that process through which the worker experiences a loss of concern for his clients, physical and/or emotional exhaustion, and a dehumanized perception of people (Maslach and Pines 1977). Burnout is found to be especially prevalent among human service workers who deal with great numbers of people who have chronic problems and little or no progress in sight (Maslach 1978). This description is relevant to the guests of a soup kitchen, most of whom have long-standing problems of a serious nature. People come to a soup kitchen for a meal, and, although some guests do "progress" in ways that a staffperson can appreciate (e.g., getting a job, stopping drinking, moving to better housing), this is not usually an expectation the guest brings with him. The guest population is therefore one that would traditionally lead to burnout, yet the staff of the Tabernacle Soup Kitchen seems less burned out than the staffs of other agencies. I find that despite all problems, the soup kitchen in many ways functions better than the usual human service, and religious motivation appears to deter burnout.

Potential Problems of Religious Motivation

A potential danger of religious motivation in soup kitchen staff is the temptation to proselytize. For example, in his study of men on skid row, Spradley (1970) states that those who eat or sleep at a skid row mission in exchange for professing religious beliefs are called "mission stiffs," denoting insincere religious participation. In her study of the treatment of skid row alcoholics, Jacqueline Wiseman (1970) describes the spiritual-religious therapy of Christian Missionaries (her pseudonym for the Salvation Army). Here, men can participate in the shelter, meals, and alcohol rehabilitation if they go to the frequent church services that sometimes include testimonies of their belief in Christ.

Because of the prevalence of a religious orientation within the soup kitchen staff, one might wonder if religious expectations are communicated to the guests. During the first two years of the Tabernacle Soup Kitchen's history, it was advertised on a sign outside the church, and in an ad in the local newspaper, as providing communion at 12:15 P.M. and a meal at 12:30 P.M. Although the communion service was held on a different floor from the dining room, and there was little effort to urge the guests to participate in it, the two issues of religion and the meal were linked in the advertisements. Few of the guests attended the services. At the time of this writing, the church was holding a 12:15 communion service only once a week, and there was no mention of it in any of the printed material of the soup kitchen.

Neither Jean nor Christine appeared to engage the guests directly in religious discussions or to proselytize. However, both directors signed their editorials about the soup kitchen that appeared regularly in a newsletter to the community *Faithfully*, and Jean signed her thank-you notes to organizations in the community *Yours in Christ*.

Are soup kitchen staffs consciously aware of the potential effects of their own religious orientation on the guests? In one discussion, a nun who is the director of another soup kitchen told me that she made it a point never to imply that any kind of religious belief or activity was tied to the soup kitchen meal. She said, for example, that whenever the dining room, which is a storefront on a street, is used for a mass for a recently deceased guest, she makes sure that the mass does not overlap with the mealtime, so that the religious service and the meal are not connected. She also said that she is aware that some guests prefer to enter the dining room only after the prayer at noon. This director appeared to feel strongly that any proselytizing of guests would be a violation of the spirit in which the soup kitchen meal should be given.

Summary

The soup kitchen staff serves those who come for a meal, as guests, not clients or patients. There is usually no implicit or explicit request for help. Many guests come because their lives are in fact on the way down, through the loss of a job, ill health, continuing or worsening alcoholism, drug addition, or mental illness. The usual source of human service gratification—improvement—does not generally occur. In addition, most soup kitchens hire few staff members, so that the camaraderie of peer support is missing. The Tabernacle Soup Kitchen, for the four years of the study, had at most two staffpersons at a time. Volunteers who help cook and clean are usually there too infrequently to be support persons for the director, and they are not sufficiently involved with the guests to feel the same frustrations.

It appears to me that the staff, in its philosophy about the soup kitchen, is successful in creating the nurturing, social, and accepting quality that makes the Tabernacle Soup Kitchen stand out from the usual array of human services. The staff lacks the usual forms of social distance from the people it serves, as well as social control over them. The staff is often alone with as many as a hundred to two hundred people at a time. In addition, the need to see "improvement" in their clients does not occur, since most of the guests are not in the soup kitchen to improve, but to eat and to socialize.

The soup kitchen is a little-explored setting in which to study issues of staff survival and development. How soup kitchen staffs work within a setting without the social distance, social control, peer support, and treatment philosophy of most other agencies is an important issue for future study.

11

Concluding Thoughts

What are we to say finally about this resurgence of soup kitchens amidst the general affluence of North American society in the latter part of the twentieth century? Are we as a people expressing some basic desire to return to the food sharing of an earlier era of human history when hunters and gatherers divided their meat and fruits with others in their band? Is the soup kitchen a response to the shock of seeing people on the streets, people who have so visibly fallen through the cracks of our fragile welfare system? Whatever its roots, the Tabernacle Soup Kitchen has gone well beyond the modest goals of offering coffee and a hot meal prepared with food salvaged from the discards of the rest of society. It has succeeded in providing a social center for a group of people who are demonstrably impoverished by all contemporary American definitions of poverty.

Attitudes About Being a Guest

Perhaps the most difficult area to explore within the soup kitchen was *how* the guests felt about being there. One might hypothesize that since the guests are a part of the dominant North American culture, with its well-known derogatory view of all forms of welfare and charity, they too would share that outlook. I had to approach this part of my exploration with caution, since I sensed that the

150

guests were indeed at least ambivalent about their own soup kitchen attendance.

Although treading on a sensitive area, I was able to gather some indirect evidence about the guests' attitudes toward their own soup kitchen participation.

Guests Outside the Dining Room

One indication of a less-than-positive feeling about being a soup kitchen guest was the reluctance of some of them to acknowledge their attendance when they were away from the dining room. As I mentioned earlier, some of the guests appeared to avoid my glance when we were back on the street, and I always respected this and also pretended that I had never seen them before. In my four years of soup kitchen participation, this nonrecognition happened frequently enough for me to think that there was a pattern to it, and that it could not be fully explained by an individual's dislike for me or by his poor memory. Rather, it appeared that the guests were not immune to the larger society's opinion of charity and a handout, and so the person would prefer not to let his soup kitchen attendance be known.

Joking in the Dining Room

Another piece of evidence that indicated the guest's sensitivity about his soup kitchen attendance was the joke "Let me buy you a cup of coffee" frequently said by one guest to another, sometimes in the semiromantic banter between men and women. The joke was a way to pretend for the moment that the soup kitchen was a commercial establishment where one buys a cup of coffee. The joke underlines the difference between a coffee shop and a soup kitchen, which is evident to everyone.

Waiting in the Soup Kitchen

Many guests had an attitude of waiting for something better to happen. Frequently heard were remarks such as "I'm waiting for my SSI (Supplemental Security Income) to come through, and then I'm splitting," or "I'm waiting for next semester to come around,

and then I'm going back to school," or "Next week I'm packing my kids and myself and we're going back to Maine." After being around the soup kitchen for several years, I began to realize that in fact many of the people never left, or, if they did leave, soon came back. It appeared that a part of these future plans was related to a story people told themselves about *why* they found themselves in a soup kitchen dining room each morning.

Stories implying temporariness are similar to the stories reported by Jack McIver Weatherford (*Porn Row* 1986). After worrying for some time about how he would explain his anthropological interest in working in a pornographic bookstore, he found that almost everyone he met on "porn row" also had a story about his reasons for being there. Weatherford, too, relates these explanations to feelings of rejection of the idea of any permanent involvement with the situation. Harley C. Schreck, Jr. (1977), in an excellent thesis on a soup kitchen in Montana in the 1970s, also discussed the aspect of waiting for something better that was reported to him by the soup kitchen guests. They, too, appeared to want to view their situation as temporary and transitional.

A Soup Kitchen Poem
My search for correspondence with guests of soup kitchens led me to a poet, Janice King, who sent me the following poem, which she wrote after eating in St. Anthony's Dining Room.

Franciscan Holiday

Robert Herrick and I went to Saint Anthony's kitchen
We without funds were fed on Thanksgiving
We met Buck and his four children
Robert pretended to be Buck's Brother, I the sister-
in-law, the 16 year old girl cousin my daughter
because Father Floyd knows Buck and his three
and we wanted to sit together. Ten young women
from Presentation High School sang for our entertainment.
Standing in line we bantered with a tall Negro busboy
telling the children about live animal donations
"We're expecting a shipment of elephants today!"

The children were alternately fighting and gay
and had good repartee with the policemen,
accused each other of spoiling the line by farting.

No cafeteria line like on other days, today we had waiters
bringing plates piled with tender turkey and dressing
We saw two piemen and a piewoman, simple Simons
bringing in our pumpkin, bringing in our donated apple
I had a scoop of eggnog icecream on my pumpkin pie
Robert had peach the old lady making a mess had berry
Robert was playing Hank Williams on his tape player
turned it off as the loudspeakers brought us *Michelle*
That is my granddaughter's name. We marched into the
kitchen to the tune of *Michelle*.
The girls from Presentation

sang Country Road, Sing a New Song, and other songs
in wild ten part harmony with two guitars accompanying
Father Floyd thanked Jesus CHRIST "whom we see in
each one of us today" and I thank the kitchen
When I'm rich again they'll get a big check from me
They did us proud today. Three hundred turkeys
went into several thousand hungry bellies for free

One thing I like about this City
is the love of Saint Anthony. (King 1978)

Miss King has not only captured some of the relaxed, bantering ambiance of a soup kitchen on a festive occasion, but I believe she has also expressed her negative feelings with the tongue-in-cheek expressions "two piemen and a piewoman, simple Simons bringing in our pumpkin, bringing in our donated apple," and the "wild ten part harmony" of the singers from Presentation High.

Guests Speaking in Public About the Soup Kitchen
One more aspect of this discussion is whether the guests see themselves as a group. I have continued to refer to the guests of the soup kitchen as a culture, though guests rarely say "we the guests" as people might say "we the Navajo" or "we the Jews." Yet, in November, 1986, when Christine asked me to be a part of a conference celebrating the five-year anniversary of the Tabernacle Soup Kitchen, we asked five of the regulars (Arnold, Marcos, Debbie, Barbara, and Esther) if they would be willing to speak about the meaning of the soup kitchen to them in front of an audience of fifty people who were college students and community workers. They agreed and were apparently willing to speak of themselves as "we the guests" at least for that occasion. The feelings they expressed were positive about both themselves and the soup kitchen, with none of the ambivalence I have described above. Perhaps the conference was couched in such positive terms that they perceived the audience to be a sympathetic one, which indeed it was.

Areas for Future Research

As a first systematic study of a soup kitchen, the ethnographic and quantitative materials presented in the preceding chapters suggest many additional areas for future study.

Guests and Nonguests

One of the unanswered questions implicit in this study is: Who *does not* come to the soup kitchen? Although we have documented the poverty of the guests of the Tabernacle Soup Kitchen, we know that there are many other people in Middle City who have the same demographic, economic, and social characteristics as the guests, but who never enter the dining room. It is important to know how the guests compare to the nonguests of Middle City. Are there people who are so poor and socially isolated that they do not know about the soup kitchen? Are there people who cannot get there, such as those living in rural poverty outside of Middle City? Are there people who are so socially timid that the specter of one hundred people in the dining room is more than they can face?

The issue of whom the soup kitchen is *not* serving lends itself to a quantitative study of a systematic sample of the poor of Middle City, followed by a comparison of the soup kitchen cohort with a non-soup kitchen cohort. One appropriate place for drawing such a sample would be in the waiting room of the general assistance office of the Town Hall, where those who exist on meager grants from public assistance sit and wait to be seen. If indeed the soup kitchen is attracting an identifiable segment of the poor, are there ways to widen its service, or is it currently doing as much as its present structure can tolerate?

Additional Services in the Dining Room?

Because the soup kitchen is successful in attracting so many of the unserved and underserved of society, there is a temptation to suggest using it for additional services to the guests. For example, we know that only a portion of those eligible for food stamps are currently receiving them. Those not receiving them come from the ranks of the street people whose lives are too chaotic to meet the challenge of eligibility requirements, or whose addresses are too unstable for the residence requirements. It is plausible to suggest that food stamp workers station themselves in the dining rooms of soup kitchens and bring that service to people in need. This same suggestion could be made for a great number of services, including health and mental health counseling, educational offerings, and housing assistance.

However, bringing in too many members of the professional world could lead to the demise of the indigenous culture that now exists. With professional services come forms, labels, lines, full-name identities, and a number of other accoutrements of modern society from which the dining room is now free. There is, it seems to me, much room for additional work to enhance the quality of life of the guests in ways that *are* paperless and hassle-free, and thus culturally congruent with the life of the soup kitchen.

The experience of the three community counseling projects within the Tabernacle Soup Kitchen suggests that there are intervention strategies that can be culturally congruent. In the years of gathering information for this study, I have observed a successful job-training program for a small group in the kitchen crew and the beginnings of a food cooperative among guests. The strategies of self-help that do not view people as incapable or as "ill" would fit well with the philosophy of the soup kitchen. There are various groups, including the Hotel Paradise men and women, the recent migrants from Puerto Rico, the young mothers and their children, and the deinstitutionalized mentally ill, that can become involved in yet untried strategies.

Types of Soup Kitchens

Another area of productive study would be a survey of soup kitchens throughout the country. How representative are the findings about the Tabernacle Soup Kitchen? Do they reflect only those in small cities of industrial New England, or is the culture of the dining room replicated in most throughout the country? A comparison of types could offer us insights into the patterns of variation in different settings and sectors of the underclass.

Nutrition

It would be beneficial to attempt more systematic diet recalls with a sample of the dining room guests, to discover how soup kitchen meals can be prepared most nutritionally. This information would be useful to the staff who plans the meals and would also be important to those who supply food for soup kitchens by food salvage. At this point, the existing literature on soup kitchens and nutrition comes from anecdotal sources of research on hunger and homelessness (Harvard University 1984).

Employment

Work is the major activity in North American culture that provides people with money, social relationships, and a sense of self-esteem. The guests of the dining room are almost all outside of the work force, being chronically unemployed. Even in periods of relatively low official unemployment, the guests are still out of work. The dining room offers the opportunity to know the chronically unemployed in a setting conducive to deeper understanding of their motivations, problems, and hopes.

Welfare

The largest group of guests received their income from general assistance known in Middle City as town welfare. This program was created by the Social Security Act as a *temporary* emergency measure. It was developed as a program for people who were between jobs or who were waiting to become eligible for another program.

In fact, most of the guests on general assistance have been on the program for at least six months, and some have been involved for years. The program is the most meager of all welfare programs; in Middle City it provided $25 a week in cash and a monthly direct payment to the landlord of $200 (usually for a room). The number of General Assistance recipients has nearly doubled nationwide from

1977 to 1983 (Stagner and Richman 1986) and so this program would be a fruitful area of further research.

Summary

Soup kitchens have reemerged in America in the 1970s and 1980s with the convergence of an increasingly disaffiliated and marginal underclass, the deinstitutionalization of the mentally ill, the shrinking of federal commitment to provide funds for people in poverty, and the growing awareness of and interest in issues of hunger and homelessness. These trends have brought soup kitchens out of America's metropolitan skid rows and into towns and small cities such as Middle City.

The study presented here has examined the impact of this renaissance on one group of soup kitchen guests. As an ethnography, it has sought to describe the daily round of life within one dining room over a four-year period. As a "natural setting," the soup kitchen has offered us a glimpse of the lives of people who are most often seen as patients, clients, or "problems" by the rest of society.

The soup kitchen offers a unique configuration of physical comforts and opportunities that compensate for the lack of human contact that most other people take for granted in work, family relationships, and consumer activities. Although perhaps initially attracted to the soup kitchen by the promise of food, the guests soon discover there a world within the dining room where the quest for sociability, acceptance, and affiliation through the formation of social networks can be fleetingly realized. The soup kitchen culture is formed as individuals learn the attributes of sociability and acceptance within the dining room. The culture is newly reenacted each day, and dissolves at a specified time, when the soup kitchen, in a manner reminiscent of Cinderella's carriage, turns into a church basement once again.

One of the contributions anthropological studies have made is in challenging stereotypical views of groups who are without power in contemporary society. An assumption regarding soup kitchens has been that their major attraction and function is to provide a hot meal for the hungry. The qualitative and quantitative data presented here go beyond the nutritional service, by refocusing our attention on the social aspects. Through a cultural understanding of the soup kitchen we can come to appreciate its value to a segment of the community.

Sociability in the soup kitchen serves the needs of people such as Sue, Marilyn, and Pedro, all of whom found in it a social center in their lonely lives. Sue, who was recovering from head injury, coma, and long hospitalization, spent over two years there, reestablishing human contact by smoking cigarettes, drinking coffee, playing solitaire, and carrying on conversations with a variety of other guests.

Marilyn used the soup kitchen for a social setting as she searched for a niche in life after a series of losses, including divorce, foreclosure on her house, and the removal of her children. She gravitated to the soup kitchen for a place to sit down, have a cup of coffee, and an occasional conversation.

Pedro also used the soup kitchen as his social center. He found the role of *Popi* to the young children of the single mothers, and was also maker of the morning coffee. He used the dining room as his morning living space, and the sidewalk in front of the Hotel Paradise as his afternoon and evening space. In both places he greeted the world and was acknowledged by those who knew him.

Beyond sociability is the atmosphere of acceptance in the soup kitchen. This acceptance means that a person like Mark, who was frantically pacing through town; or Steven, who was laughing to himself and talking of the drowning babies and open electrical circuits all around him; or Madeline, who wove her way through traffic and pleaded for money, are not shoved aside but are seen as "belonging" within the dining room. Although Mark, Steve, and Madeline might not often be engaged in the sociability of the rest of the soup kitchen, they appeared to know that it was a place where they would not be laughed at or looked at clinically, and where they could enjoy several hours of just being themselves. In this way, the soup kitchen has accomplished something positive in the otherwise dismal world of the deinstitutionalized mentally ill.

The soup kitchen is also able to provide some measure of social support through the social networks that are formed in the dining room. The middle-aged women who are no longer married and whose children are gone from them form one group. Another network is formed by the young single mothers, their babies and toddlers, and some of their male friends. The young women of the Hotel Paradise form another group, as do the young Hispanic men of the hotel. The boundaries of each group are fluid, and the soup kitchen dining room is one of the few examples in modern life where a great deal of socializing happens across age, sex, and ethnic divisions among groups that may otherwise be isolated from, or even hostile to, each other.

The naturally forming social networks within the dining room have important implications for people who establish social policy and who are interested in improving the quality of life of the poor. These social networks are untapped resources for enhancing the degree of support that members can give each other. One approach is to provide some members of each network with information about community resources which they and their friends may utilize. Much can be done to encourage formation of social networks within the dining room, and to disseminate information and resources through those networks.

Soup kitchens have reappeared in American society in a period of public reconsideration of society's obligation to those who cannot survive in the competitive, job-oriented, postindustrial society that requires relatively high levels of skill and knowledge. The fact that the chronically unemployed and the physically and mentally ill are not reaping the bounty of affluence is increasingly thought of as "not our problem" by society's leaders. This attitude is visible in the decreasing commitment to financing social programs, and there is now even discussion of reduced spending for the once-sacrosanct Social Security and Civil Service retirement benefits (Pear 1986: 4E).

In contrast, the Tabernacle Soup Kitchen offers the guests refuge and asylum for a few hours a day, and its philosophy enables an indigenous culture to grow and flourish. We have been able to demonstrate how this culture promotes an ambiance in which the dining room provides an oasis for its guests in an otherwise hostile or indifferent world.

References

Allport, G.
   1954   *The Nature of Prejudice.* Garden City, N.Y.: Doubleday Anchor Books.
American Diabetes Association Inc.; American Dietetic Association
   1976   *Exchange List for Meal Planning.*
Appleby, L., N. Slagg, and P. Desai
   1982   The Urban Nomad: A Psychiatric Problem. *Current Psychiatric Therapies* 21:253–61.
Auletta, K.
   1982   *The Underclass.* New York: Vintage.
Axinn, J., and H. Levin
   1975   *Social Welfare: A History of the American Response to Need.* New York: Harper and Row.
Aykroyd, W.
   1975   *The Conquest of Famine.* New York: Reader's Digest Press.
Baasher, T.
   1983   On Vagrancy and Psychosis. *Community Mental Health Journal* 19(1):27–41.
Bachrach, L.
   1980   Overview: Model Programs for Chronic Mental Patients. *American Journal of Psychiatry* 137(9):1023–31.
   1984   Research Devices for the Homeless Mentally Ill. *Hospital and Community Psychiatry* 35(9):910–13.
Bahr, H.
   1973   *Skid Row: An Introduction to Disaffiliation.* New York: Oxford University Press.

Barnes, J.
    1954   Class and Committees in a Norwegian Island Parish. *Human Relations* 7(1):39–58.
    1972   Social Networks. An Addison-Wesley Module in Anthropology. Module 26:1–29.
Bass, P.
    1983   Heavier Burden of Poverty for New Haven. *New York Times*, July 24:22 Section II.
Baxter, E., and K. Hopper
    1981   *Private Lives/Public Spaces: Homeless Adults on the Streets of New York City.* New York: Community Service Society.
Behrhorst, C.
    1975   The Chimaltenango Development Project in Guatemala. In Kenneth Newell, ed., *Health by the People.* World Health Organization 30–51.
Bell, D.
    1973   *The Coming of the Post-Industrial Society.* New York: Basic Books.
Bernard, J.
    1973   *The Sociology of Community.* Glenview, Ill.: Scott Foresman.
Bierman, E.
    1982   Obesity. In J. Wyngaarden and L. Smith, eds., *Cecil Textbook of Medicine.* Philadelphia: W. B. Saunders 1372–79.
Blaustein, A., ed.
    1982   *The American Promise.* New Brunswick, N.J.: Transaction.
Bogdan, R., and S. Biklen
    1982   *Qualitative Research for Education.* Boston: Allyn and Bacon.
Bohannan, P.
    1981   Natural History of a Research Project. In D. Nesserschmidt, ed., *Anthropology at Home in North America: Methods and Issues in the Study of One's Own Society.* Cambridge: Cambridge University Press.

Bott, E.
    1957   *Family and Social Network*. 2nd ed. London: Tavistock.
Boujouen, N., and J. Newton
    1984   *The Puerto Rican Experience*. Willimantic, Conn.: Wind-
            ham Regional Community Council.
Britan, G.
    1978   The Place of Anthropology in Program Evaluation. *Anthro-
            pological Quarterly* 51:119–28.
Broomfield, B.
    1985   Personal communication with caseworker at North East Ac-
            tion Community.
Cobb, S.
    1976   Social Support as a Moderator of Life Stress. *Psychoso-
            matic Medicine* 38:300–14.
Cohen, N., J. Putnam, and A. Sullivan
    1984   The Mentally Ill Homeless: Isolation and Adaptation. *Hos-
            pital and Community Psychiatry* 35(7):922–24.
Combs, B.
    1985   Personal communication with official of the Salvation Army.
Connecticut Food Bank
    1985   Feeding the Needy of Connecticut—Slim Pickin's.
Conrad, P., and J. Schneider
    1980   *Deviance and Medicalization: From Badness to Sickness.*
            St. Louis: C. V. Mosby.
Cowen, E., et al.
    1979   Hairdressers as Caregivers I. *American Journal of Com-
            munity Psychology* 7(6):633–48.
Cox, D.
    1984   Soup Kitchen Open to All for a Day. *New York Times*,
            November 18, Conn. Section:25.
Day, P.
    1981   *Social Work and Social Control*. London: Tavistock.
Dietrich, J.
    1985   Miracle of Hope. *Catholic Agitator* 15(3):3.

Dinitz, S., R. Dynes, and A. Clarke
   1975   *Deviance: Studies in Definition, Management and Treatment.* 2nd ed. New York: Oxford University Press.

Dohrenwend, B. and B.
   1969   *Social Status and Psychological Disorder: A Causal Inquiry.* New York: Wiley-Interscience.

Dukert, J.
   1983   Who Is Poor: Who Is Truly Needy? *Public Welfare,* Winter:17–22.

Dumont, M.
   1967   Tavern Culture: The Sustenance of Homeless Men. *American Journal of Orthopsychiatry* 37:938–45.

Edgerton, R.
   1967   *The Cloak of Competence: Stigma in the Lives of the Mentally Retarded.* Berkeley: University of California Press.

Eisenberg, L.
   1977   The Search for Care. In J. Knowles, ed., *Doing Better and Feeling Worse: Health in the United States.* New York: W. W. Norton.

Farb, P., and G. Armelagos
   1980   *Consuming Passions: The Anthropology of Eating.* Boston: Houghton Mifflin.

Faulkner, L., W. Terwilliger, and D. Cutler
   1984   Productive Activities for the Chronic Patient. *Community Mental Health Journal* 20(2):107–22.

Firth, R.
   1973   *Symbols: Public and Private.* Ithaca, N.Y.: Cornell University Press.

Foster, G.
   1969   *Applied Anthropology.* Boston: Little, Brown.

Freeman, J.
   1979   *Untouchable: An Indian Life History.* Stanford, Calif.: Stanford University Press.

Fried, M.
1975   Social Differences in Mental Health. In J. Kosa and I. Zola, eds., *Poverty and Health*. Cambridge, Mass: Harvard University Press.

Furstenberg, F., and A. Crawford
1978   Family Support: Helping Teenage Mothers to Cope. *Family Planning Perspective* 10(6):332–33.

Giachello, A., et al.
1983   Use of the 1980 Census for Hispanic Health Services Research. *American Journal of Public Health* 73(3):266–74.

Glasser, M.
1976   Incidence of Psychiatric Problems in One Family Practitioner's Practice. *Journal of Family Practice* 3(5):558–59.

Glave, J.
1983   Meese's Comment Means Little to Those with Nothing. *Journal Enquirer*, December 10.

Goffman, E.
1961   *Asylums*. Garden City, N.Y.: Doubleday.

Goldsmith, D., et al.
1985   An Anatomy of Loitering: Social Behavior Around Methodone Programs. Unpublished paper.

Goodenough, W.
1957   Cultural Anthropology and Linguistics. In P. Garvin, ed., *Report of the Seventh Annual Round Table Meeting on Linguistics and Language Study*. Washington, D.C.: Georgetown University Monograph Series on Language and Linguistics (9).
1971   *Culture, Language and Society: A McCaleb Module in Anthropology*. Addison-Wesley.

Handel, G.
1982   *Social Welfare in Western Society*. New York: Random House.

Harrington, M.
1962   *The Other America*. New York: Macmillan.

Hartford, M.
  1971   *Groups in Social Work*. New York: Columbia University
         Press.
Harvard University School of Public Health
  1984   *American Hunger Crisis: Poverty and Health in New
         England.*
  1985   *Physician's Task Force on Hunger in America.*
Health System Plan for Eastern Connecticut, 1979–1983.
Henderson, J.
  1981   Nursing Home Housekeepers: Indigenous Agents of Psy-
         chosocial Support. *Human Organization* 40(4):300–05.
Hombs, M., and M. Snyder
  1972   *Homeless in America: A Forced March to Nowhere*. Wash-
         ington, D.C.: Community for Creative Non-Violence.
Horn, J.
  1969   *Away with All Pests*. New York: Modern Reader.
Hymes, D.
  1969   The Use of Anthropology: Critical, Political, Personal.
         Reinventing Anthropology, D. Hymes (ed.), New York:
         Pantheon Books.
Jaynes, G.
  1981   Urban Librarians Seek Ways to Deal with Disturbed Pa-
         trons. *New York Times*, November 27, Section A:16.
Jochim, M.
  1981   *Strategies for Survival: Cultural Behavior in an Ecological
         Context*. New York: Academic Press.
Kammerman, S.
  1980   Social Policy and the Poor: Fact and Fiction. *Public Wel-
         fare*: Fall 38:21–25.
Kaplan, D., and R. Manners
  1972   *Culture Theory*. Englewood Cliffs: Prentice Hall.
Keefe, T.
  1984   The Stresses of Unemployment. *Social Work* May–June
         264–68.

Kenen, R.
1982   Soap Suds, Space and Sociability: A Participant Observation of the Laundromat. *Urban Life* 11(2):163–83.
King, J.
1978   Franciscan Holiday. Dial Designates, collection of unpublished poems.
Kohrs, M., et al.
1979   The Association of Obesity with Socioeconomic Factors in Missouri. *American Journal of Clinical Nutrition* 32:2120–28.
Konrad, G.
1969   *The Case Worker.* New York: Harcourt Brace and Jovanovich.
Kosa, J., and I. Zola, eds.
1975   *Poverty and Health.* Cambridge Mass.: Harvard University Press.
Lamb, H.
1979   The New Asylums in the Community. *Archives of General Psychiatry* 36:129–34.
1984   Deinstitutionalization and the Homeless Mentally Ill. *Hospital and Community Psychiatry* 35(9):899–906.
Langness, L.
1965   *The Life History in Anthropological Science,* G. and L. Spindler, eds., New York: Holt, Rinehart and Winston.
Lawrence, F.
1986   Personal communication with native Swedish speaker.
Leach, J.
1979   Providing for the Destitute. In J. Wing and R. Olfsen, eds., *Community Care of the Mentally Disabled.* New York: Oxford University Press.
Lerner, M.
1975   Social Difference in Physical Health. In J. Kosa and I. Zola, eds., *Poverty and Health.* Cambridge, Mass.: Harvard University Press.

Levitan, S.
  1978 *Programs in Aid to the Poor for the 1970s* (rev. ed.). Baltimore: Johns Hopkins University Press.
Lewis, O.
  1966 *La Vida*. London: Panther Books.
Liebow, E.
  1967 *Tally's Corner: A Study of Negro Street Corner Men*. Boston: Little, Brown.
Loewenstien, G.
  1985 The New Underclass: A Contemporary Sociological Dilemma. *Sociological Quarterly* 26(1):35–48.
Lovell, A.
  1978 From Confinement to Community: The Radical Transformation of an Italian Mental Hospital. *State and Mind*, Spring 7–11.
McElroy, A., and P. Townsend
  1979 *Medical Anthropology*. Belmont, Calif.: Wadsworth.
Maguire, L.
  1983 *Understanding Social Networks*. Beverly Hills, Calif.: Sage.
Malone, M.
  1979 Old and on the Street. *Aging* 281–92:21–27.
Maslach, C.
  1978 The Client Role in Staff Burn-Out. *Journal of Social Issues* 34:111–24.
Maslach, C., and A. Pines
  1977 The Burn-Out Syndrome in the Day Care Setting. *Child Care Quarterly* 6:100–13.
Mehrabian, A.
  1976 *Public Places and Private Spaces: The Psychology of Work, Play and Living Environments*. New York: Basic Books.
Mehrabian, A., and J. Russell
  1975 Environmental Effects on Affiliation Among Strangers. *Humanitas* 11:219–30.

Merry, S.
  1981   *Urban Danger: Life in a Neighborhood of Strangers*. Phil-
         adelphia: Temple Press.
Mitchell, J., ed.
  1969   *Social Networks in Urban Situations*. Manchester, Eng-
         land: Manchester University Press.
Mitchell, R., and E. Trickett
  1980   Task Force Report: Social Networks as Mediators of Social
         Support. *Community Mental Health Journal* 16(1):27–44.
Moubray, C.
  1985   Homelessness in America: Myths and Realities. *American
         Journal of Orthopsychiatry* 55(1):4–8.
Murray, H.
  1984   Time in the Streets. *Human Organization* 43(2):155–61.
Myerhoff, B.
  1978   *Number Our Days*. New York: Simon and Schuster.
Myrdal, G.
  1962   *Challenge to Affluence*. New York: Pantheon Books.
Nanda, S.
  1984   *Cultural Anthropology* (2nd ed.). Belmont, Calif.:
         Wadsworth.
New, P., and Y. Cheung
  1984   The Evolution of Health Care in China: A Backward Look
         to the Future. *Medical Anthropology* 8(3):169–71.
Newsweek
  1986   Abandoned. January 6:14–19.
New York Times
  1986   Homeless and Hungry Found in Worse Plight. January 21,
         Section A:18.
Patton, M.
  1986   Personal communication with director, Connecticut Food
         Bank.
Pear, R.
  1986   Chipping Away at the Idea of "Entitlement." *New York
         Times*, February 9, Section E:4.

Pelto, P. and G.
   1970   *Anthropological Research: The Structure of Inquiry* (2nd ed.). Cambridge, Mass.: Cambridge University Press.

Peplau, L., and D. Perlman
   1982   Perspectives on Loneliness. In L. Peplau and D. Perlman, eds., *Loneliness: A Sourcebook of Current Theory, Research and Therapy*. New York: Wiley.

Perloff, H.
   1982   *Critical Issues for National Urban Policy: A Reconnaissance and Agenda for Further Study*. Washington, D.C.: National Academy Press.

Peters, T.
   1985   Why Smaller Staffs Do Better. *New York Times* April 21, Section 1:14–15.

Piven, F., and R. Cloward
   1971   *Regulating the Poor*. New York: Vintage Books.

Poverty in the Region
   1980   Report of the Regional Planning Agency.

Preston, S.
   1984   Children and Elderly in the United States. *Scientific America* 251(6):44–49.

Redick R., and M. Witkin
   1983   *State and Country Mental Hospitals, US 1970–1980 and 1980–1981 Mental Health Statistical Note 165*. Rockville, Md.: National Institute of Mental Health, August.

Regional Planning Agency of Middle City
   1980

Rendle, G.
   1984   Welfare, Charity and Ministry: Postures in the Helping Relationship. *The Christian Century*, May 2:464–67.

Roberts, N.
   1984   *Dorothy Day and the Catholic Worker*. Albany: State University of New York Press.

Rosenthal, M., and J. Greiner
  1982 The Barefoot Doctors of China: From Political Creation to Professionalization. *Human Organization*, Winter 1982, 41:330–41.

Rousseau, A.
  1981 *Shopping Bag Ladies: Homeless Women Speak About Their Lives.* New York: Pilgrim Press.

Rubenstein, C. and P. Shaver
  1982 The Experience of Loneliness. In L. Peplau and D. Perlman, eds., *Loneliness: A Sourcebook of Current Theory, Research and Therapy.*

Schaefer, C., J. Coyne, and R. Lazarus
  1981 The Health-Related Functions of Social Support. *Journal of Behavioral Medicine* 4(4).

Schensul, S. and J.
  1978 Advocacy and Applied Anthropology. In G. Weber and G. McCall, eds.; *Social Scientists as Advocates: Views from the Applied Disciplines.* Beverly Hills, Calif.: Sage.

Scheper-Hughes, N.
  1982 Anthropologists and the "Crazies." *Medical Anthropology News* 13(2):1–2, 6–11.
  1983 A Proposal for the Aftercare of Chronic Psychiatric Patients. *Medical Anthropology Quarterly* 14(2).

Schreck, H.
  1977 Structure Versus Nonstructure at the Poverello Center. Unpublished Master's Thesis, University of Montana.

Segal, S., and J. Baumohl
  1980 Engaging the Disengaged: Proposal on Madness and Vagrancy. *Social Work* 25(5):358–65.
  1982 The New Chronic Patient. In L. Snowden, ed., *Reaching the Underserved.* Beverly Hills, Calif.: Sage 95–113.

Shapiro, J.
  1969 Dominant Leaders Among Slum Hotel Residents. *American Journal of Orthopsychiatry* 39:644–50.

Sheehan, S.
  1982 *Is There No Place on Earth for Me?* New York: Vintage
        Books.
Sherman, H.
  1976 *Stagflation: A Radical Theory of Unemployment and Infla-
        tion.* New York: Harper and Row.
Sherraden, M.
  1985 Chronic Unemployment: A Social Work Perspective. *Social
        Work* 30:403–408.
Sidel, V., and R. Sidel
  1973 *Serve the People.* Boston: Beacon.
  1982 *The Health of China.* Boston: Beacon.
Slater, P.
  1970 *The Pursuit of Loneliness: American Culture at the Break-
        ing Point.* Boston: Beacon.
Snowden, L.
  1982 Services to the Underserved. In L. Snowden, ed., *Reach-
        ing the Underserved.* Beverly Hills, Calif.: Sage.
Spradley, J.
  1979 *The Ethnographic Interview.* New York: Holt, Reinhart
        and Winston.
  1970 *You Owe Yourself a Drunk: An Ethnography of Urban
        Nomads.* Canada: Little, Brown.
Stack, C.
  1975 *All Our Kin: Strategies for Surviving in a Black Commu-
        nity.* New York: Colophon Books.
Stagner, M., and H. Richman
  1986 Reexamining the Role of General Assistance. *Public Wel-
        fare* Spring 40:20–32.
Stern, M.
  1984 The Emergence of the Homeless as a Public Problem. *So-
        cial Service Review,* June:291–301.
Stuart, R., and B. Davis
  1972 *Slim Chance in a Fat World.* Champaign, Ill.: Research
        Press.

Suchman, E., B. Phillips, and G. Streib
  1958   An Analysis of the Validity of Health Questionnaires. *Social Forces* 36:223–32.
Talbott, J.
  1979   Deinstitutionalization: Avoiding the Disaster of the Past. *Hospital and Community Psychiatry* 30:621–24.
Tissue, T.
  1972   Another Look at Self-Rated Health Among the Elderly. *Journal of Gerontology* 27(1):91–94.
Torrey, E.
  1969   The Case for the Indigenous Therapist. *Archives in General Psychiatry* 20:365–73.
Turner, J., and A. Maryasnski
  1979   *Functionalism*. Menlo Park, Calif.: Benjamin Cummings.
Van Putten, T.
  1976   Drug Refusal in Schizophrenia and the Wish to be Crazy. *Archives in General Psychiatry* 33:1443.
Walker, K., A. MacBride, and M. Vachon
  1977   Social Support Networks and the Crisis of Bereavement. *Social Science and Medicine* 2:35–41.
Wallace, A.
  1970   *Culture and Personality* (2nd ed.). New York: Random House 1970.
Weatherford, J.
  1986   *Porn Row*. New York: Arbor House.
Weicher, J.
  1984   *Maintaining the Safety Net*. Washington, D.C.: American Enterprise Institute for Public Policy Research.
Weil, W.
  1984   Demographic Determinants of Obesity. In D. Kaller and M. Sussman, eds., *Obesity and the Family*. New York: Haworth 21–32.
Whyte, W.
  1943   *Street Corner Society*. Chicago: University of Chicago Press.

Wiesenfield, A., and H. Weis
  1979   Hairdressers and Helping: Influencing Behavior of Informal
          Caregivers. *Professional Psychology*, December 10:787–92.

Wiseman, J.
  1970   *Stations of the Lost: The Treatment of Skid Row Alcohol-
          ics*. Englewood Cliffs, N.J.: Prentice Hall.
  1979   Close Encounters of the Quasi-Primary Kind. *Urban Life*
          8:23–51.

Wolfe, A.
  1978   The Use of Network Thinking in Anthropology. *Social Net-
          works* 1(1):53–64.

Wolff, K. ed.
  1950   *The Sociology of George Simmel*. New York: Macmillan.

Yeh, S., and B. Chow
  1972   Nutrition, Medicine and Public Health in the People's Re-
          public of China. In *Medicine and Public Health in the
          People's Republic of China*. Washington, D.C.: U.S. Gov-
          ernment Printing Office 215–39.

You-Long, G., and C. Lin-Min
  1972   The Role of Barefoot Doctors. *American Journal for Public
          Health* 72 (Supplement):59–60.

Index

Acceptance of guests, 8, 10, 11, 13, 86, 87, 91, 94, 96, 100, 120, 138, 158, 159; as deprofessionalism, 10–11; as benevolent anarchy, 10–11; as a reason for going to the soup kitchen, 88–95
Advocate and advocacy, 46, 126, 143
Affiliation. *See* Sociability; Social networks; Social relationships
AIDS: the potential of prevention, 136. *See also* Self-help
Alcoholism, 3, 39, 42, 112, 117; alcoholic, 39, 71, 95, 103, 132; delirium tremems, 91; alcohol counselor, 125, 131, 132. *See also* Drinking
Anthropologist(s), 43, 48, 81; medical anthropologists, 53
Anthropology, 4, 43, 44, 47, 52, 152, 158; urban anthropology, 4–8, 43; applied anthropology, 48
Appleby, Lawrence, 98
Armelagos, George, 10
Asylum, 11, 87, 88, 92, 94, 161
Auletta, Ken, 7
Aykroyd, W., 15–16

Bachrach, L. L., 20, 87, 88
Barnes, J. A., 12
Basaglia, Francisco, 98
Baxter, E., 5, 42, 78, 85
Behrhorst, Carroll, 119
Bell, Daniel, 7
Bierman, Edwin, 59

Biklen, Sari Knopp, 127
Blaustein, Arthur, 18
Bogdan, Robert, 127
Bohannan, Paul, 43
Boredom in the soup kitchen, 113, 121, 131, 134, 137
Bott, E., 12
Boujouen, Norma, 55
Britan, Gerald, 127

Catholic Worker Movement, 139. *See also* Ministry; Staff
Charity, 22, 150
Cheung, Y., 119
Child abuse, 43, 83, 94, 106, 115, 124, 130, 132, 134; failure to thrive, 114; children removed from home, 55, 95, 113, 114; protective service worker, 135
Children in the soup kitchen, 55, 72, 73, 74, 79, 93, 95, 101, 105, 109, 110, 111, 113, 114, 123
Christian church, 22; Saint Mary's Church, 23–30. *See also* Ministry; Religion
Christianity, 26–27, 139, 141, 147–48
Clarke, A., 98
Cloward, Richard, 119
Cobb, S., 117
Companionship, 10, 42, 85
Conrad, Peter, 145
Cowen, Emory, 120

Coyne, James, 11, 101, 103
Crime, 86; arrests, 94–95, 104, 132; criminal charges, 98; criminal acts, 99. See also Prison
Cultural relativism, 99
Cultural themes, 8–12
Culture of poverty, 6–7
Culture of the soup kitchen, 4, 48, 136, 154, 159, 161

Day, Dorothy, 139
Deinstitutionalization of mentally ill, 17, 20, 22, 87, 88, 156, 158, 159
Demographic characteristics of guests: age, 47, 50, 54; sex (gender), 47, 53; ethnicity, 47, 50; household membership, 47; educational level, 50, 63. See also Guests
Depression, Great, 14. See also Soup kitchen: historical references to
Desai, Prakash, 98
Deviance, 86, 88, 98; deviant, 86; medicalization of, 145
Dinitz, S., 98
Dohrenwend, Barbara, 60
Dohrenwend, Bruce, 60
Drinking, 42, 59, 72, 83, 134, 145; drunk, 79, 91, 110. See also Alcoholism
Drug use, 9, 86, 121; heroin, 71; getting high, 38, 72, 112, 136; drugs, 42, 59, 79, 94, 124, 132, 142; cocaine, 104; drug counselor, 125; drug dealer, 146
Dumont, M. P., 3, 103, 108
Dynes, R., 98

Ecological niche, 2
Education, 47, 50, 63; General Education Diploma, 115; English as a Second Language class, 53, 55, 63
Eisenberg, Leon, 60
Emic and etic distinction, 34–35

Emotional support, 101, 106, 107, 110, 116, 117
Employment. See Work
Ethnicity, 47, 50
Ethnographic methods, 12
Ethnography, 34–35, 43, 55, 158

Family relationships, 37–38, 74–75, 95, 105–07, 111–12, 113–16, 135
Farb, Peter, 10
Food, 10, 20, 28, 29, 37, 143, 158; soup kitchen meal, 9–10, 30; food salvage, 28, 150; feeding ministry, 30; attitude toward, 74; appetite, 76, 143; food sharing, 150. See also Nutrition
Food Stamps, 21, 111, 150, 156
Foster, George, 48
Freeman, James, 42

Gatekeepers, 44–46
General Assistance. See Welfare
Gheel, Belgium, 98
Giachello, Aida, 31
Glasser, Morton, 60
Goffman, Erving, 144–45
Goldsmith, Douglas, 9
Goodenough, Ward, 4
Grenier, Jay, 118
Guests: as soup kitchen nomenclature, 3; as a social status, 27, 133; as key informants, 37–41; attitude toward being a guest, 42, 150–54; world view of, 35, 78; a "regular" guest, 121, 123, 129, 154. See also Demographic characteristics of guests

Harrington, Michael, 139
Hartford, Margaret, 122
Health, 47, 55, 58–63; access to health care, 47, 62–63; indigenous health workers, 119
Health problems, 1, 55, 58–63, 70, 71, 72, 73, 74, 78–79, 80, 84, 85, 159;

physical disabilities, 40, 81, 82, 83, 86, 92–93, 98, 99; dental problems, 62. *See also* Mental health problems; Psychiatric
Henderson, J. Neil, 119, 120
Hispanic, 28, 31, 32, 50, 53, 55, 64, 126, 160. *See also* Puerto Rican
Hombs, Mary Ellen, 98
Homeless, 5, 17, 20, 21, 41, 42, 77, 108, 122; awareness of homelessness, 21–22, 158; shelters, 5, 78, 95
Hopper, Kim, 5, 42, 78, 85
Horn, Joshua, 118
Housing, 32, 47, 56–57, 75, 77, 112; cooking facilities in, 52. *See also* Single-room-occupancy hotel (SRO)
Human service, 33, 68, 123, 144, 145, 149. *See also* Social work
Hunger: awareness of, 21–22, 158
Hungry, 17, 23, 52
Hymes, Dell, 48

Income, 47, 55–56; loss of, 85. *See also* Work
Indigenous leadership, 35, 111–13, 118, 131, 136
Indigenous workers, 118–20, 121, 124, 127, 129
Italian Democratic Psychiatry Movement, 98

Joking, 111, 151. *See also* Guests

Kammerman, Sheila, 17, 19
Kaplan, David, 99
Keefe, Thomas, 19
Kenen, Regina, 8, 9, 69
King, Janice, 153

Lamb, Richard, 20, 88
Langness, L. L., 42
Lazarus, Richard, 11, 101, 103
Leach, J., 98

Leaders. *See* Indigenous leadership
Lerner, Monroe, 62
Levin, H., 16
Levitan, Sar, 19
Lewis, Oscar, 6
Liebow, Elliot, 3, 5
Life history method, 42
Li Min, Chao, 118
Loneliness, 48, 69, 70–84, 116, 117, 121; lonely, 81, 82, 85, 100; "loners," 120, 136. *See also* Social isolation
Lovell, A., 98
Lowenstein, Gaither, 7

McElroy, Ann, 62
Manners, Robert, 99
Marginality, 3, 20, 48, 158
Maslach, Christina, 147
Mehrabian, Albert, 9
Mental health problems, 20, 55, 58–62, 73, 74, 77, 84, 86, 87, 89, 90, 91, 98, 99, 126, 132; "crazy," 81; mentally ill, 87, 88–92, 160; disorientation, 97; psychotic, 121; bizarre behavior, 126, 128. *See also* Psychiatric; Health
Ministry, 138–41; City Ministry Committee, 23–24, 27, 45; "living the gospel," 24; minister, 126. *See also* Religion
Mitchell, J. Clyde, 11
Mitchell, Roger E., 12, 117
Myerhoff, Barbara, 6, 35, 116
Myrdal, Gunnar, 6

Nanda, Serena, 122
New, P., 119
New England, 3, 8, 33, 156
Newton, James, 55
Nutrition, 26, 28, 52, 65–67; nutritionist, 66, 125, 131, 157

Participant observation, 34–35, 103; issues in, 41–44

Patton, Mark, 22
Pelto, Gretel H., 35
Pelto, Pertti J., 35
Peplau, Letitia, 69
Perlman, Daniel, 69
Phillips, B. S., 58
Physical disabilities. See Health
Pines, Agula, 147
Piven, Frances Fox, 119
Poor: of Middle City, 31–32; invisibility
    of, 31; urban, 85
Postindustrial society, 6, 160
Poverty, 17–19, 21, 24, 31, 48, 56, 62
Preston, Samuel, 19
Prison, 39, 73, 85, 133; probation, 90;
    jail, 37, 95. See also Crime
Proselytizing. See Religion
Psychiatric, 11, 38, 40, 60, 62, 70, 75,
    77, 87, 89, 97, 126, 132. See also
    Mental health problems
Puerto Rican, 30, 31, 37, 39, 41, 50, 70,
    78–81, 90–91, 94, 107, 111, 112, 122,
    123, 131, 140, 156. See also Hispanic

Qualitative research methods, 12, 34–
    35, 103, 159
Quantitative research methods, 12, 34–
    35, 46–47, 48, 50, 96, 159

Redick, R. W., 20
Religion: religiosity, 11; religious com-
    munity, 21; Christianity, 26, 27; Jew-
    ish community, 28; Bible study, 74,
    110; religious motivation, 140, 141,
    143, 147–48. See also Ministry
Rendle, Gilbert, 139
Rituals of soup kitchen, 4
Roberts, N., 139
Rosenthal, Marilyn, 118
Rousseau, Ann Marie, 3, 88
Rubenstein, C., 121
Russell, James, 9

"Safety net" programs: shrinkage of, 17,
    20–21
Salvation Army, 14
Sanctuary, 11, 87
Schaefer, Catherine, 11, 101, 103, 117
Scheper-Hughes, 10, 11, 98
Schneider, Joseph, 145
Schreck, Harley C., 152
Self-help, 12, 118–21, 130, 137, 156;
    community counseling class as, 40,
    41, 46, 83, 94, 121–37, 156; potential
    in AIDS prevention, 136
Shapiro, Joan, 103, 107
Shaver, P., 121
Sheehan, Susan, 87
Shelter, 5. See also Homeless
Sherman, Howard, 19
Sherraden, Michael, 19
Sidel, Ruth, 118, 119
Sidel, Victor, 118, 119
Simmel, Georg, 8, 9
Single-room-occupancy hotel (SRO), 32,
    43, 57, 75, 95, 103, 108, 128; Hotel
    Paradise, 71, 72, 78, 79, 81, 90, 94,
    97, 110, 112, 123, 160; "thieves' den,"
    73, 89
Slagg, Nancy, 98
Slater, Phillip, 3
Smoking as an issue in the soup
    kitchen, 96
Snyder, Mitch, 98
Sociability, 8–10, 11, 13, 69, 85, 87,
    120, 138, 158
Social center: soup kitchen as a, 5, 116;
    Jewish Community Center as a, 5, 6,
    116
Social control, 138, 144–46, 149; social
    distance, 145
Social isolation, 41, 98, 117, 132, 155;
    sitting alone, 82, 91; speaking to no
    one, 88. See also Loneliness
Social networks, 8, 11–12, 100–117, 120,
    122, 130, 136, 158, 160

Social relationships, 84, 85, 90, 100; social interaction, 72, 85, 132
Social support, 11, 13, 103, 104, 107,
115, 116. *See also* Emotional support
Social work, 46; social service, 53, 55,
63; social workers, 53, 81, 90, 91,
125. *See also* Human service
Soup kitchen: as an ecological niche, 2;
as a "problem free" service, 3, 96–97;
social functions of, 8, 52; rules of, 11,
97; as a model of service, 12; a renaissance of, 14, 49; as barometers of
poverty, 14; definition of, 15; historical references to, 15–17; Soup
Kitchen Act of 1847, 15; soup kitchen
protocol, 36–37; utilization of, 47, 52,
64–65; future research in, 155–58
Sponsorship of the soup kitchen, 28–29.
See also Ministry
Spradley, James, 4, 5, 34
Staff: benevolent anarchy, 10; deprofessionalism, 10, 11; directors, 26–27,
141–44; philosophy, 138–41; peer support, 146; burnout, 147. *See also* Ministry; Religion
Stern, Mark, 21
Streib, G. F., 58
Subculture, 4. *See also* Culture of the
soup kitchen
Suchman, E. A., 58

Tally's Corner, 3, 5
Tissue, Thomas, 58
Townsend, Patricia, 62
Trickett, Edison, 12, 117

Underclass, 6, 7–8, 17–20, 138, 158;
new underclass, 7
Unemployed, 7, 19–20, 52, 55, 130, 157,
160; unemployment, 8, 17, 22, 24, 42,
43

Violence, 2, 41, 43, 106, 134, 146
Volunteers, 26, 27, 30, 84, 111, 133,
139, 142, 143

Wallace, Anthony F. C., 4
Weatherford, Jack McIver, 152
Weis, Herbert, 120
Welfare, 2, 13, 18, 27, 32, 38, 55, 56,
74, 75, 82, 109, 112, 125, 129, 133,
144, 150, 157; Aid to Families of De-
pendent Children (AFDC), 55, 75,
119; General Assistance, 55, 75, 85,
89, 98, 155, 157; Supplemental Secu-
rity Income, 55
Whyte, William Foote, 5
Wiseman, Jacqueline, 85
Wisenfeld, Alan, 120
Witkin, M. J., 20
Wolfe, A. A., 12
Wolff, K., 8
Work: relationship of guests to, 56, 63–
64, 72, 73, 83, 90, 93, 110, 112, 113,
122, 128, 129, 135, 157
Workfare, 26, 27, 30, 38, 39, 41, 53, 56,
78, 90, 92, 93, 104, 111, 123, 128,
135, 142, 143, 144

You-Long, Gonag, 118